Ethics of speech communication

THE BOBBS-MERRILL SERIES IN *Speech Communication*

RUSSEL R. WINDES, *Editor*
Queens College of the City University of New York

THOMAS R. NILSEN

University of Washington

Ethics of speech communication

SECOND EDITION

The Bobbs-Merrill Company, Inc.
INDIANAPOLIS AND NEW YORK

Editor's foreword

Ethics is that branch of the humanities studying values which relate to human behavior. Students of ethics concern themselves with the rightness and wrongness of human behavior, and also with the goodness and badness of the motives and results of behavior. Presumably whenever and wherever human behavior affects the lives of others certain "rules" of conduct and moral obligation become significant. Communication, as a primary instrument of human behavior, pervasively touches and affects the lives of others. Therefore, the argument goes, communication, if it is to contribute to the growth of society, must be associated with and governed by ethics. If such is not the case, the power of communication will be used by self-seeking and self-serving individuals and groups for essentially destructive ends.

If one agrees to this concept of the role of ethics in communication, then it follows that underlying both the teaching and learning of speech communication there must be a recognition and concern about the motivations of the communicator (and his auditors) and the potential influence of his message on himself and his receiver. Two issues consequently follow, both vital: Should one accept the conclusion that communication without an associated ethical structure is dangerous? If a system of ethics is desirable, or necessary, what ethical system based upon what values can best produce morally acceptable communication?

Those who advocate leashing communication to an enforceably strong value dimension point with considerable anxiety to the shocking events of the past decade, its confrontations, protests, and violence, as awesome examples of the results of divorcing communication and rhetorical theory and processes (including media) from socially responsible values. They cite cases of unprincipled individuals and organizations, within government and without, engaging in devious and deceptive rhetoric to create situations so intensely emotional that the rational processes of deliberation and conflict resolution have been, at times, totally unable to function. The victims of such evil, all of us, are unable to deal judiciously and calmly with such communication behavior because, in practice, we were never taught how to do so. We were never told that the power to do good was also the power to do evil. Because in our studies of communication we continually assessed rhetoric as an amoral discipline, unrelated to ethics, we became unwilling servants to the will of others, nearly helpless before the threats and intimidations of the demagogues. An amoral discipline has contributed handsomely to the Age of Anxiety in which an extensively fragmented, inflamed, and despairing society could not get a grip on itself.

These charges, even if exaggerated, cannot be dismissed lightly. Perhaps our approach to the study of communication has become as obsolete and dangerous as our approaches to economics, diplomacy, and ecology. Those who believe this is true in our discipline have found their scapegoats—the rhetoricians blame the behaviorists; the behaviorists blame the rhetoricians. Both may be right. Students of speech have long been accused of lack of concern over questions of the ethical use of theories generated by their research and observations. In earliest times the study of rhetoric suggested an essentially amoral discipline, one concerned with the acquisition of gambits which could easily be used by the sophist, or the demagogue, to manipulate and control society to evil ends. Although rhetoricians spoke often of the ideal orator as a good man speaking well, far more attention was given to "speaking well" than to "the good man." In recent years, with the scientific study of communication—persuasion and propaganda, manipulation of public opinion, refined systems of motivational analysis—which the rhetorician has embraced, the image of speech communication as a potential weapon in the arsenal of the demagogue has loomed larger in the intellectual community. The science of rhetoric has developed rapidly, but associated study in the value dimensions of rhetoric has been almost nonexistent.

One of the important criticisms of behaviorists in speech communication has been that they have introduced into the study of rhetoric a nonvalue, nonethical approach and methodology. They have participated successfully in the development of a "science" of communication that seeks to change environment, not people, that seeks to alter actions, not feelings, that shifts the customary psychological emphasis on the world inside man to the world outside him. As a result, many argue, the view of man as the initiator, the originator, the creator, the agent responsible for his own behavior and its impact on others has become fiction. Autonomous man has become a myth, and along with autonomous man, any system of ethics in which he may have believed. Thus, it can be said that the student of speech communication is not concerned with enabling his fellowman to communicate justly, honestly, and wisely, relating his communication to feelings and concerns about the betterment of mankind. The behaviorist is little concerned with the use of communication in moral struggles or in building inner virtue. He has created a technology that distorts his humanity. He is the scientist who seeks truth regardless of morality or ethics; communication is a phenomenon to be observed, studied, investigated without concern over its ultimate use for good or evil.

Given these criticisms, it is little wonder that the image of the discipline comes to be that of a study lacking ethical dimension; little wonder that the concept of the student of speech communication has come to be that of the technician who naively formulates ever more sophisticated programs for mass control—at best a Bruce Barton, at worst a Goebbels. In our desire to become an important part of the academic mainstream we may have helped to develop the Bomb and the Bomb's delivery capacity, but we have not yet developed the humanistic values which alone can advise us on the use of the weapon.

The results can be, may have been, tragic. Without the guidelines and their commitments to human dignity and freedom, an irresponsible and undisciplined rhetoric may already have become both coercion and anarchy, contributing to the loss of dignity and freedom. Moreover, the movement away from responsible communication may have accelerated during the past decade to the degree that widespread abuse cannot now be controlled. B. F. Skinner, of late a very troubled behaviorist, put the problem well in his utopian **Walden Two:**

> At this very moment enormous numbers of intelligent men and women of good will are trying to build a better world. But problems are born faster than they can be solved. Our civilization is running away like a frightened horse . . . and as she runs her speed and her panic increase together. As for your politicians, your professors, your writers, let them wave their arms and shout as wildly as they will. They can't bring the frantic beast under control.

Many scholars in speech communication are deeply concerned with bringing "the frantic beast under control." This may not be evident to the undergraduate. Because of his expectancy, and perhaps his cynicism, the novice might well recognize only the pragmatic aspects of speech communication, all the while ignoring the broader implications of the ways in which these concepts must be used to increase the freedom of the individual and improve the quality of human life. There is, we believe, implicit concern in the Bobbs-Merrill Series in Speech Communication with values and ethical applications: How can speech promote the growth and self-realization of the individual? How can speech promote a free society in which each member has equal justice and equal opportunity? How can speech be used in society to redress grievances, correct injustices, and produce needed change without becoming the exclusive tool of those who believe in neither justice nor freedom? These issues are significant throughout the Series. In addition to these ethical concerns, however, we believed at the inception of this Series that it was important to devote an entire volume to issues which were implicit in the other volumes, to set forth in an organized manner a view of the ways in which speech communication ought to be employed and studied for the betterment of mankind.

Professor Nilsen's **Ethics of Speech Communication** remains the first and only book in the discipline devoted to the relationships between communication and ethics. He presents an answer to those who eschew the study of communication in favor of a simplistic concept which stresses the honest individual sincerely speaking to an audience endowed with common sense. By stressing the subtlety of the speech communication situation, the difficulty in determining what the truth is and when it ought to be used, and the varied and complex ways our messages affect others, this book suggests a reappraisal of many of our "common sense" ideas about what constitutes ethical speech. Professor Nilsen states well the nature of the book:

> This is a book on the ethical use of words; it is practical ethics, making no pretense of developing theory. It assumes an ethical system which places the human personality at the center of values. The purpose of the book is not to formulate a set of prescriptions for morally right speech, but to attempt to indicate what such a value system implies for communication, and to suggest some principles of communication that are important to the preservation and the more complete realization of the values of a free society. The central theme of the book is the importance of the self-determining personality and the moral obligation to contribute to its growth through what we do and say.

Although the basic approach to the second edition of **Ethics of Speech Communication** remains essentially the same as the first edition (1966), Professor Nilsen has updated the book to include discussions of ethical problems of protest and confrontation and to recognize the moral problem facing the minority that seeks to shake an unresponsive bureaucracy from its lethargy:

> I have tried to recognize that at times an element of coercion may be justified in righting wrongs, in achieving greater equality. But I have tried to emphasize, too, that coercion cannot be legitimized as a principle of social change in democratic society, and that coercive rhetoric places upon those who use it a peculiar moral burden which may not be taken lightly. I have tried to recognize the value of the increased awareness of the role of feeling in human life, yet realizing that in a complex world feeling alone, however sensitive and compassionate, is not sufficient basis for moral conduct.

Professor Nilsen's volume should be must reading for those who, like myself, believe we can no longer afford the luxury and foolishness of an amoral discipline. We must shape a new ethic for speech communication which honors the human dimension and which makes rhetoric our servant not our master.

                                                              Russel R. Windes

Preface

> Respect for the word is the first commandment in the discipline by which a man can be educated to maturity—intellectual, emotional, and moral.
>
> Respect for the word—to employ it with scrupulous care and incorruptible heartfelt love of truth—is essential if there is to be any growth in a society or in the human race.
>
> To misuse the word is to show contempt for man. It undermines the bridges and poisons the wells. It causes Man to regress down the long path of his evolution.[1]

Through words we affect the well-being of others, in peculiarly subtle and significant ways—in private life where personality touches personality, and in the public arena where issues affecting the life of society are decided.

This is a book on the ethical use of words; it is practical ethics, making no pretense of developing theory. It assumes an ethical system which places the human personality at the center of values. The purpose of the book is not to formulate a set of prescriptions for morally right speech, but to attempt to indicate what such a value system implies for communication, and to suggest some principles

[1] Dag Hammarskjöld, **Markings** (New York: Knopf, 1965), p. 112.

xii   *Ethics of speech communication*

of communication that are important to the preservation and the more complete realization of the values of a free society. The central theme of the book is the importance of the self-determining personality and the moral obligation to contribute to its growth through what we do and say.

The volume is oriented toward the student of speech communication; the material should be an integral part of the theory and principles of speech making, informal discussion, and interpersonal communication. Speaking is not limited, quite obviously, to students in classes in speech communication. Wherever people talk to people, ethical principles are of vital importance, both to the development of free, self-governing personalities and to the strengthening of our free, self-governing society.

Ethical principles alone, however, are not sufficient for moral conduct. "Morals," as Mark Van Doren said, "cannot be better than thought. The soundest method of moral education is teaching how thought is done."[2] And Erich Kahler wrote, "In times like these, decent behavior is no simple matter, for it is no longer merely a moral, but also a mental, task. It requires a highly developed intellectual faculty, the ability to grasp the very complex social situation of a closely interrelated nation and world, a task so difficult that people abandon it and relapse into the moral and social anarchy of today."[3] But it also seems plain, more than ever today, that developing the intellectual faculty or getting training in "how thought is done" does not automatically result in morally right action. What is needed is probably best summed up by A. E. Morgan:

> We must have free, critical, objective inquiry, without boundaries or pre-commitment or qualification—though not without humility and a sense of proportion; and we must have passionate, whole-hearted commitment to the best we know, again with humility and a sense of proportion. Too often we have thought of critical inquiry and moral enthusiasm as mutually exclusive. Only to the extent that they are organically united do we have the conditions essential for the preservation of democracy and freedom.[4]

Thomas R. Nilsen

[2] Mark Van Doren, **Liberal Education** (Boston: Beacon, 1959), p. 63.
[3] Erich Kahler, **Man the Measure** (New York: George Braziller, 1956), p. 17.
[4] A. E. Morgan, "Ethics and the Functioning of Democracy," in **The Scientific Spirit and Democratic Faith;** papers from the Conference on the Scientific Spirit and Democratic Faith, New York, May 1943 (New York: King's Crown Press, 1944), p. 26.

Contents

1. *An ethical orientation* 3

Ethical problems in communication, 5
The bases of our ethical judgments, 11
Clarification of terms and concepts, 15
Ethics and speech, 17
Related readings, 20

2. *On telling the truth* 21

Truth telling, values, and language, 22
Applications of the concept of truth telling, 27
On trying to tell the truth, 40
Related readings, 42

3. *On significant choice* 43

Significant choice and the ethics of speech, 43
The criterion of significant choice, 46
Significant choice and the marketplace of ideas, 53
Motivation to significant choice, 55
Self-understanding and significant choice, 55
Emotion and significant choice, 57
Related readings, 59

4. *On persuasion*   *60*

The course of action and the speaker's moral obligations, 61

The means of persuasion and the speaker's moral obligations, 65

The ethics of information, 71

The ethics of reasoning, 76

Related readings, 83

5. *On the "optimific" word*   *84*

On whether we should always do the best we can, 84

On opportunities for saying the better thing, 88

Related readings, 96

6. *"In times like these . . ."*   *97*

Related readings, 106

Index of names, 107

Subject index, 109

Ethics of speech communication

ONE

An ethical orientation

As a subject of study ethics deals with questions of right and wrong conduct, of the good and the bad, and of moral obligation. In one sense we all know a good deal about such questions, but in another sense we know very little. Without any formal study of ethics we can all point to or describe many acts we would unhesitatingly call wrong, and others we would call right. We all feel there are some things we **ought** to do, and some things we **ought not** do. We ought to help people we encounter who are in need; we ought to keep our promises, be helpful, civil, and avoid hurting others. We ought not cheat, slander, deceive, or otherwise injure another human being. In short, we feel we ought to do what is right, and we ought not do what is wrong.

We are aware, however, that it is often difficult to decide whether an act or statement is morally right or wrong. We are frequently unsure of ourselves when trying to decide what is, in a given case, the right, or good, or better thing to say or do. For instance, is it wrong to tell a lie to avoid hurting someone's feelings? To be honest, must we tell the "whole truth" about what we are talking about? If we present only "facts," are we being truthful? Is it wrong to break a window or two in order to call attention to what we are saying about an important social problem that people in authority seem to be ignor-

3

ing? Is it wrong to use obscene language when our intentions are good (even if the obscene language offends some people)? If we are selling something, whether an artifact or an idea, ought we tell about its weaknesses as well as its strengths? Ought we to go out of our way to say or do the right thing? Can we really know, in most cases, what is the morally right thing to do or say?

We could go on to ask why we should be good in the first place—that is, whether there are any but prudential reasons why we should be—but this would take us into an area of ethical theory beyond the scope of this book. We shall accept the virtually universal assumption that we ought to do what is morally right, if we can know what it is.

The questions raised above suggest that ethical questions are not confined to issues of great moment, but arise constantly in our day-to-day living, whenever the behavior—verbal or nonverbal—of one person affects the well-being of another. The philosopher Ralph Barton Perry states, "The moral drama opens only when interest meets interest; when the path of one unit of life is crossed by that of another."[1] Most human actions, then, are part of a moral drama, since almost everything said or done by one person touches the life of another. From the small courtesies that make human relations more pleasant to the supreme sacrifice of one life for another, what one human being does affects the well-being of others. The eloquent phrases of an inspired leader may energize a nation; a thoughtless remark may injure the feelings of a sensitive child. Over the whole range of human life, words have their impact on people for good or ill.

Our concern in this book is with the ethics of speech communication; that is to say, we are concerned about the effect that the speaking of one person has on the well-being of those touched by it, directly or indirectly, immediately or at a later time.[2]

---

[1] Ralph Barton Perry, **The Moral Economy** (New York: Scribner, 1909), p. 13.
[2] Our concern in this volume is not to elaborate ethical theories, but we should note that if we accept this concept of the good as a basis for ethical judgments, we are committing ourselves to a teleological or utilitarian theory of ethics. Generally, such a theory states that the basis for judging an act to be good is whether it contributes to a balance of good over evil. In other words, the act is judged in terms of its consequences or in terms of rules which are based on the probable consequences of such acts. In contrast to the teleological theories are the formalistic or deontological theories, which state that the rightness or wrongness of an act does not depend upon its effects but upon whether the act conforms to an ethical rule or principle. For example, calling an act right because it

In this chapter we will point up some of the ethical problems presented by various forms of communication, discuss briefly the value system which underlies the basic ethical questions we raise about communication procedures, clarify terms used, and present the general orientation of the book toward the study of the ethics of speech communication.

Ethical problems in communication

When we think about the "ethics of speech," what probably first comes to mind is political campaigns and quasi-political protests and demonstrations. This is not surprising, since in a democratic society political campaigns are an essential and recurring feature of national life, from the election of the village mayor to the election of the nation's President. And where traditional political processes fail to meet the needs of significant groups in society—as they see these needs—extrapolitical means are used, and since their success is in large part dependent on the attention they get, such tactics are employed as will get the most of it.

In citizen political action the interests of literally hundreds of different social, economic, labor, and professional organizations are involved, and so too is the personal success of the competing politicians. In other words, the stakes are high for the many and diverse individuals and groups taking part; and with it all, the opportunities for deception and guile, for manipulation and influence peddling, are endless. Moreover, our political tradition has legitimized a kind of public symbolic infighting and given license to accusation, exaggeration, and partisanship such as is rarely tolerated outside the political arena.

Even though we may discount much of the "campaign oratory," we are faced with the fact that in political campaigns significant issues are often avoided or oversimplified and attention-getting but minor issues are often exaggerated. Vague fears are heightened, fears of the culprits of the season, whether they be fascists or communists,

---

is in accord with God's will, irrespective of its consequences, is strict deontologicalism.

It seems probable that all ethical principles grew out of a recognition of the results of various forms of behavior, and that there is, as a consequence, a vestige of teleology in deontological theories. For a brief account of major ethical theories, see, for example, W. K. Frankena, **Ethics** (Englewood Cliffs, N.J.: Prentice-Hall, 1963).

capitalists or labor leaders, student activists or revolutionary pro-
fessors. A political slogan or "formula" is sought which captivates
public interest and creates a sense of common purpose, yet does not
raise serious questions about difficult problems.

A thoughtful and humane person cannot but feel grave doubts about
whether this is the way to decide who will have the power to make war
or peace, to decide whether we will feed our hungry and clothe our
poor, whether we will put men to work. Is this the way to develop informed and critical citizens who can make intelligent choices?

Where the well-being of many is so vitally involved, our ethical
common sense tells us that it is morally wrong to evade issues, to
present highly biased and misleading information, to oversimplify
problems, and to place the success of a political party above the
opportunity for genuine choice on the part of the voters. Where such
important decisions are to be made, there is, we cannot but feel, a
moral obligation to have more respect for truth, more honesty and
candor in the discussion of issues, and more selfless interest in the
public good.

However, when we consider some other factors, such as the practical problems faced by the candidate, we may be less certain in our
moral criticism. If a candidate were to attempt to discuss the intri-
cacies of policy, would he lose the interest of his audience? Would
he open himself to objections and criticisms to which he would
have no opportunity to reply? Moreover, if he did not talk about those
things of most interest to each particular group of listeners, in terms
familiar to them, would they listen? If he did not try to reassure
the voters of his common humanity and sincerity, thus enabling them
to identify with him, could he be elected?

These questions do not lessen the moral obligations of the candidate; they do not change the ethical issues. They do, however, remind
us how difficult it is to know what is the most morally right thing to
do or say in a given case. Campaign speaking and the public-relations
activity that goes with it are important to the democratic process. Such
speaking provides at least some basis upon which voters can have
confidence in their choice of a leader, and some basis upon which
to approve or disapprove the general directions of public policy. To
say and do that which best serves the public good is difficult indeed,
especially under the pressures of a campaign.

As mentioned above, when the ordinary and accepted political processes appear to be dominated by vested interests and the existing institutions are seen as unresponsive to the needs of significant numbers of people, other methods of social change are sought. Recent years have seen a particularly active period of protest against inadequately responsive and allegedly inhumane institutions—educational, political, legal, economic—and there has been violent outcry for greater opportunity and equality. Protest has taken many forms, from peaceful sit-ins, teach-ins, mass meetings, and boycotts, to mass confrontations, traffic-disrupting marches, and physical attacks on property and persons. The speaking has varied as greatly, from the religiously oriented exhortations to nonviolent resistance of Martin Luther King, Jr., to the virulent, often obscene and profane denunciations and attacks of some of the more radical leaders of such groups as the SDS, the Weathermen, and the early Black Panthers. The earlier protest urged legal and political action in the accepted tradition; the later and more radical protest often repudiated the traditional legal and political methods in favor of demands backed by coercive power.

The protest movement in the large has had as its goal the eradication of social injustice. It has not always been clear that some of the more militant leadership has been so committed. Inevitably it seems that a social movement seeking radical changes attracts to it individuals of such extreme views and temperament that they distort the aims and actions of the movement itself.

The problem of achieving greater equality and justice is made more difficult by other types of extremists, those who seem to oppose all social change. Whether to preserve their own vested interests—economic, political, or cultural—or because of religious or other ideological conviction, they condemn virtually all social legislation or cultural change, most of which is seen as the machinations of a diabolical communism. For many people such right-wing extremism gains a certain validity with its appeal to tradition, religious fundamentalism, and the preservation of law and order.

It is easy to become morally indignant, and not without reason, when groups flout established authority and custom and seem to foster a disrespect for law and normal democratic political procedures, which the majority feel to be the very bases of their social, political, and economic security. But when one sees the disparity between rich and poor, black and white, privileged and underprivileged, and when the political processes are seen as radically favoring the white and the affluent (as can be seen in tax laws, selective law enforcement, partisan legislation) it is not surprising that the disadvantaged—and those in deep sympathy with them—should seek to force social change. The built-in bias in legal codes and political processes leans toward the preservation of the existing legal, political, and economic relationships; and the inertia of a culture preserves its values even though the natural and technological environment may be changed. Where the disparity, the discrimination, the disadvantage is arbitrary, it is hard to condemn the aggression that stems from the frustration of those who feel outraged and see normal avenues of change as blocked.

At the same time, however, it is difficult to countenance actions that seem to endanger the very institutions which make constructive social change possible—which make possible the greater realization of the goals of equality and justice. Thus we live with an ethical dilemma that man has faced, in all probability, since organized society has existed.

Although political campaigns and organized protest are spectacular examples of public communication that raise ethical questions, such campaigns and protests do come and go. There are other significant public communications, however, with which we are unremittingly confronted through the mass media: advertising, news, entertainment of every description, preaching, and pressure-group propaganda.

Advertisements too often mislead by implying much more than they explicitly claim. They appeal to vanity and cupidity; they play on the emotions surrounding the need to have the approving attention of others. Advertisements sometimes display and glamorize products that are demonstrably harmful. In their endless appeal to self-glorification and aggrandizement they distort our sense of values.

Newspaper reporting is often extremely biased; some events and issues are ignored or suppressed while others are exaggerated, with little regard for the need for public understanding. Often headlines are lurid, stories and pictures are sensationalized, and privacy is invaded. The responsibility for informing the public is neglected.

Television programs feature crime and violence; the gun is too often the ultimate arbiter of disputes. Many shows are puerile, their production guided almost solely by the money to be made in pandering to the lowest common denominator of public taste. Responsibility for public enlightenment and cultural development is all but ignored. The commentator who arouses serious economic and political controversy, however enlightening, is likely to be replaced by the safe and innocuous television personality who avoids confronting his listeners with significant discussion.

Here, as in the case of political speaking, the ethical issues are complex. The freedom to make, to buy and sell, within broad limits, are freedoms important to a democratic society. Advertising, with all its faults, is important to a free economy. If a free economy is important to democracy, then it would appear that advertising should not be entirely eliminated. Although there is little doubt that some advertising is unethical, who can decide at what point it becomes morally wrong? How far could we go in restricting advertising without doing more harm than good? So too with respect to the communications of the press, radio, and television. At what point would restrictions and regulations make such inroads on the freedom of expression as to weaken democratic processes and undermine basic values? As much as we may lament the low standards of communication in the mass media and their failure to meet the moral obligations of public service, we must recognize that the ethical problems involved do not admit of easy answers.

There are other sources of questionable public communication. Throughout our society there are hundreds of partisan voices vying to be heard and to influence the thought and action of citizens. Every profession, every trade, almost every interest has its national and local organizations which seek to serve the interests of its members through building favorable public attitudes and influencing public policy. Every ideology, every political, social, economic, and religious persuasion, seeks to influence and proselytize. In the work of these groups there are varying degrees of public service, but there is also much that is highly partisan and self-seeking.

It is part of our heritage of beliefs, however, that such competing groups, when free to pursue their own ends, will in the long run contribute to the public good. If the competition is open, it is believed, those groups will win support which have the most to offer, and the public good will best be served. That there is truth in this is attested to by the success of our own society, in which freedom to pursue individual and group interests has been unparalleled. It is also true, however, that the exhortations and propaganda of these groups often severely distort the truth through their highly biased selection of facts and interpretations of events. Often public confusion results from the conflicting claims and demands, as, for example, in the demands of business and labor. In the case of more extreme groups, such as those of the extreme political right and left, not only do they create confusion, but worse, they sow suspicion of and create hatred toward whatever groups or individuals hold differing views.

Whatever abuses of the right of free speech may occur, we still do not want to restrict the right of people to organize in pursuit of their interests and to express themselves freely. Ethical questions cannot help arising, however, if we have any commitment to the basic values of our culture. The question is not whether freedom of speech and association serve our values: Such a freedom is at the very foundation of those values. The question is whether the widespread abuse of the freedom endangers the freedom itself by eroding the conditions that make it possible. Do extreme bias, marked lack of objectivity, disregard of sound evidence and reasoning, and crass self-interest undermine the democratic process, create disrespect for and intolerance of differing opinions, and militate against respect for the individual?

A relatively new—in terms of effectiveness—set of pressure groups has begun competing for the attention of government and society. The recent upsurge of action on the part of ethnic minorities has brought new and often strident voices into the public discourse. Where such ethnic and culturally disadvantaged minorities are concerned, their problem has been to find a voice that can and will be heard. Theirs is less a seeking of special privilege than a seeking to share the privileges they see as their due as citizens of an affluent society, to share the advantages deemed legitimate for the average member of the cultural majority. And these are not merely material advantages, but the right to be thought of and acted toward as a complete human being and citizen, without discrimination of any kind. Where there exists bias, overstatement, ethnocentricism, bitterness, or virulence, these must be viewed in the light of the peculiar circumstances of the group. This, of course, should be done for all individuals and groups; we see the need more clearly, however, where disadvantaged minorities are concerned.

It is not only in public discourse, in political campaigns, in the use of the mass media, or in the exhortations and machinations of pressure groups that ethical problems in communication are to be found. In our day-to-day interactions with others we affect them with our words in countless ways. We touch their lives by our small talk, our courtesies, explanations, instructions, entreaties, commands, words of endearment or resentment, approval or rebuke. Words as expressions of thought and feeling are instruments of action. With them we are constantly and inevitably doing things to people. Thus there is even an ethical problem in the way we use speech in our everyday lives: a failure to speak when someone needs encouragement; a hasty response that suggests indifference; an arbitrary order that wounds someone's ego; a seemingly innocent remark that hurts someone's pride; a word of disapproval in a context that magnifies the disapprobation; gossip; a half-truth, or the full truth at the wrong time or place. We cannot, of course, know at all times what effect our words will have, and sometimes a well-intentioned statement causes someone to suffer. It is not always easy to say the right thing.

This brief reflection on the ethical problems of speech should remind us of how pervasive they are and how difficult of resolution. It should also remind us that we do have a common background of values in the light of which we can make ethical judgments. Very likely there has been, thus far in this discussion, a reasonably adequate meeting of minds between reader and writer on what is morally questionable in communication and what is morally desirable, and on how difficult it sometimes is to decide which is which. If we were to make judgments about specific instances, however, we would doubtless find ourselves in disagreement very quickly.

The bases of our ethical judgments

Everyone of normal intelligence and personality structure has had a sense of right and wrong for all of his remembered life. From infancy each individual lives in an environment in which some forms of behavior are encouraged or permitted, and other forms discouraged or forbidden. The latter are usually emphasized more than the former. Some behavior is discouraged because it is dangerous to health or safety, or disturbing to others, or an inconvenience to parents, or because it differs from conventional patterns of behavior, or violates accepted moral codes. Some behavior is forbidden on religious grounds.

Out of the many "do not's," verbally and nonverbally expressed, especially those that come from parents and other family members, and to some extent from teachers and leaders or supervisors of childhood activities—the authority figures in the child's life—the conscience develops. Since the regulators of behavior influence the child from babyhood on, and are a pervasive part of his conscious and unconscious experience throughout his childhood, a sense of right and wrong becomes an integral part of his attitudinal structure. Since the concepts of right and wrong tend to be reasonably uniform in any particular culture, they tend to be reinforced in various areas of experience. In times of rapid social change this is, of course, less true.

The child has not lived very many years, however, before he begins to realize that the early arbiters of his morals do not themselves always do what is right or even know what is right. They do not agree among themselves, and from time to time they change their minds. So, as the child matures, he comes to realize that the good and the bad are not clear and fixed categories. What may be considered right at one time may be thought wrong at another. It is not so much that the basic value or ideal changes as that its application to and relevance for specific acts changes. Further, what is right in one culture may be wrong in another. The laws themselves, which reflect attempts to codify behavior so that organized communities can function, vary from place to place and are often changed and adapted to new circumstances. Religious institutions often modify their moral prescriptions from generation to generation as they attempt to apply basic religious principles to changing social conditions. The changing attitudes toward divorce and birth control are but among the most notable in this generation. Marked changes occur in customs of work and play, dress, courtship, and expression. While each older generation tends to protest against such changes as reflecting a decline in moral standards, to the new generation they are a liberation from outworn restrictions, exhilarating at first, but soon becoming commonplace.

It is small wonder that problems of good and bad, right and wrong, are difficult for everyone and have engaged the energies of thoughtful men for as long a time as we have any records of their thinking. In spite of the philosophic problems and the practical difficulties of applying ethical standards to specific instances of conduct, all societies have, in response to the needs of organized living, developed highly intricate ethical systems. While in their daily living most men are only dimly aware of the ethical principles that guide them, these principles are an integral part of their social selves. They reflect a basic attitude toward man, as well as a complex pattern of customary and habitual ways of responding, sanctioned by society. A look at simple everyday behavior and at the basic institutions of our society will reveal much about the underlying ethical principles.

If you walk down a hall or a street and someone bumps into you, you may be annoyed. If he quickly says, "Oh, I'm sorry," you will as quickly reply, "That's all right," and promptly forget the incident. If, on the other hand, he simply glares at you or avoids looking at you or talking to you, your annoyance lingers and you walk on thinking of the boorishness of some of your fellowmen. But why the difference in your response? The answer is obvious: In the first instance the person bumping you revealed a respect for you as an individual, for your personality; in the second instance he did not. It is as simple as that, but very significant nevertheless. Again, suppose you are waiting your turn at a store counter or filling station, and the clerk or attendant hails you with an "I'll be with you as soon as I can"; you feel much better about the waiting. You feel less frustrated and annoyed than if you had not been recognized. Once more the factor of respect and concern for you makes the difference. Even though you may realize that the "I'll be with you as soon as I can" is a standard phrase the personnel department has instructed the attendants to use, and may reflect little genuine sympathy, you still feel better. You realize that someone is aware of the feelings people have about being kept waiting and the indignity of being ignored.

Most of our customs about courtesy, tactfulness, or good manners—what we generally call considerateness—are based on respect for others, on a sense of their worth as individuals and their equality with us. Further, the fact that we expect similar courtesies in all human interaction emphasizes the fundamental dignity and equality we see in man.

If we move from the level of the customs of day-to-day relationships to the basic laws and institutions of society, we find the same fundamental concept of the individual. While we may be far from realizing our ideals, the Declaration of Independence does assert that life, liberty, and the pursuit of happiness are inalienable rights. The Constitution is oriented toward providing a basis in law for these rights. Although we have not thus far secured it, in full, our legal system postulates equality before the law for all who come under its jurisdiction. Our laws stipulate freedom of speech and association (within the broadest limits) for all, and prescribe self-government for men through freely elected representatives. Our educational institutions are committed, in theory if not always in accomplishment, to the concept of the equality of opportunity and the right of each individual to develop his potentials. In our generation we are attempting, if hesitatingly and haltingly, to proclaim that all men are entitled to freedom from want and fear, insofar as these can reasonably be assured by public action.

Underlying our individual behavior as well as the functioning of our social institutions is a basic conception of man. Each man, we have assumed, is a being of intrinsic worth, a being with a capacity for reason, for understanding, and for emotional and esthetic appreciation. It is this conception of the nature of man that gives rise to the corollary belief that each person should have the opportunity to develop his physical, intellectual, emotional, and spiritual potential. We believe that each man should have the maximum opportunity for self-determination, consistent, of course, with self-determination for others. We recognize that man is essentially a social being; he does not develop his distinctive characteristics in isolation. He cannot develop his full potential unless he is an integral, participating member of a creative, cooperative, and reasonably harmonious community. The community, we believe, should exist for the purpose of the optimum development of the individual.

The foregoing statement about the value of the personality and the concept of man on which our social institutions are based and which gives them direction, points to the concept of the good which characterizes our culture: Whatever develops, enlarges, enhances human personalities is good; whatever restricts, degrades, or injures human personalities is bad.[3]

As indicated above, we recognize that this concept of the good is

---

[3] It is the author's view that there are also ethical questions relative to the effects on the speaker himself of his own communicating. These will not be explicitly discussed in this volume, but the reader is urged to consider the implications of this point of view.

far from being consistently or adequately implemented in our society; it is far from being translated into universal experience. In fact, it probably never will be. Given the imperfect nature of man's understanding, the frailty of his individual will and of his institutions, we must always expect a gap between ideals and their attainment, between principles and their application. Nonetheless, we must also understand that the ideals reflect genuine beliefs, intentions, and aspirations. They reflect what we in our more calm and thoughtful moments think ought to be, however aware we may be of our actual, or even our potential, level of achievement. Our ideals provide an ultimate goal, a sense of direction, a general orientation, by which to guide conduct.

A definition of the good as that which enhances human personalities is, of course, so broad and inclusive a statement that it evokes general agreement. There is bound to be much disagreement about the definition of terms and the application of the principle to specific instances of behavior.

Clarification of terms and concepts

Thus far we have used the words "good" and "bad," "right" and "wrong," much as we use them in everyday speech, assuming, with considerable justification, that we know what they mean. Let us now define these terms more carefully. By "the good" is meant that which contributes to the well-being of man. The state of well-being is one in which the needs of the personality are being satisfied and its potentialities are being realized. In any particular case a good act is one which maximizes the state of well-being. We shall think of this state as being good. By "the bad" is meant that which reduces or destroys well-being. The state of reduced or lesser well-being we shall think of as being bad or less good. The term "right" is used to refer to actions that maximize the good, and "wrong" to apply to actions that reduce good. "Morality" as here used pertains to the making of decisions between right and wrong. A moral decision is one involving a decision between right and wrong actions. Morality implies an active agent with intentions, and the opportunity for choice. A nonmoral decision is one that does not involve a moral issue—that is, rightness or wrongness in the ethical sense. The terms "moral" and "ethical" are used virtually synonymously. By "ethics" as a subject of study is meant systematic thinking and theorizing with respect to questions about good, right and wrong, and moral obligation.

The concepts of right and wrong imply the notion of "ought." We ought to do what is right; we ought not to do what is wrong. This is the ethical sense of "ought." The term is used in various ways, and it is valuable to keep some of the more important distinctions in mind. If, for example, one painter says to another that he ought to use darker colors in his painting, he is concerned not with a moral but with an esthetic "ought." If we say that we ought to walk more carefully across busy streets or work more efficiently, we are talking mainly about prudential considerations—that is, considerations of legitimate self-interest. Certainly such actions may have moral implications. If someone whose family is dependent upon him endangers his life unnecessarily, or if by working inefficiently one person restricts another's opportunity, moral issues arise.

There is also a distinction between the legal and the moral "ought." We ought to obey the law; law-abiding behavior is expected and necessary in a civilized community. There is a distinctly prudential aspect to this obligation, but one need not look far to find an ethical aspect as well. Since laws are essential to the kind of society in which men can enjoy reasonable equality of opportunity to achieve well-being and happiness, we have a moral obligation to be law-abiding.[4]

[4] For additional distinctions among various uses of "ought," see for example Harry L. Hollingsworth, **Psychology and Ethics** (New York: Ronald Press, 1949), pp. 8–17.

Problems arise with respect to laws that no longer reflect the attitudes of the community and laws that perpetuate injustice. The so-called blue laws (laws pertaining to Sunday observance) are an example of the former. Our obeying or not obeying them has little effect on anyone's well-being; one might say that the net effect of ignoring them—which we all do—may be to promote happiness. The response to this view might well be, however, that the principle of obedience to law is important; if one disobeys even unnecessary and outdated laws, one is reducing respect for law in general and thus working against the long-term interests of the community.

Laws that discriminate against minority groups are examples of those which perpetuate injustice. There are those who argue that we have a moral obligation to oppose or break such laws. If attempts to change them through established procedures are not successful within a reasonable length of time, it may be morally right to force change by resisting the laws. There are moral grounds for this if our ultimate criterion of the good is the welfare of man.

The student interested in this problem may wish to read some discussions of it. See, for example, the essays on justifiable disobedience in R. M. MacIver, ed., **Conflict of Loyalties** (New York: The Institute for Religious and Social Studies, 1952), and Abe Fortas, **Concerning Dissent and Civil Disobedience** (New York: New American Library, 1968).

We can readily distinguish between moral and nonmoral acts by definition, but in life situations the distinction is less easy. The disposition or intentions of the doer, as we have said, are a vital part of the moral nature of his behavior. To use a simple example: A little old lady walking across a street is engaging in a nonmoral act. A young man walking across the street, by chance beside her, is acting nonmorally. If, however, he deliberately walks beside her to make her crossing easier in the midst of traffic, he is acting morally, and rightly. Thus, his walking across the street at a particular time for a particular purpose may be a moral act. On the other hand, if the young man escorts the lady across the street for the purpose of impressing onlookers, he would not be thought of as acting rightly, in the moral sense. The act might still be a good one in that it contributes to the lady's well-being, but this would be incidental to the other motive. Here we have a case of mixed motives, and the act would have to be thought of as a mixture of right and wrong—a condition true of a great many, if not most, human acts.

It is apparent that it is often very difficult for an observer to make a judgment about the moral quality of another person's actions; only rarely can the true intentions behind them be known. This is not to say that intention is the only factor, or even the major one, contributing to the ethical nature of an act. The view taken here is that it would be totally unjustifiable to consider an act as morally right in spite of its destructiveness if only the doer professed good intentions, because in making such judgments we must ordinarily assume that the doer has considered the possible consequences of his actions—anything less than this would in itself be morally wrong.

Ethics and speech

Our concern is with the ethics of speech. Every act of speech is essentially a social act, influencing the attitudes or behavior of others. Therefore, rather than attempt to divide communication into moral and nonmoral, we will think of every communicative act as having an ethical component—as carrying some degree of ethical charge. Virtually every act of speech, then, involves an ethical obligation.

Speech communication is related to so many facets of man's life that a comprehensive view of man and a far-reaching ethical concern are necessary to an adequate ethic of speech. Melvin Rader's state-

ment on the requirements of an ethic complete enough to serve man
is helpful:

> The real subject of value is the person-in-society, and this social
> personality, as a dynamic focus of interests, is the whole man. Only an
> ethics that does justice to every essential side of human nature, as both
> individual and social, as mind and body, as thinking and feeling, and
> desiring, is complete and complex enough to be the basis of valid
> ideals.[5]

Our goal as individuals and as members of groups ought to be to
act in our personal relationships with others, and through whatever
public agencies are available to us, to contribute directly and indirectly to doing "justice to every essential side of human nature."

Morally right speech, like any morally right behavior, is that which
contributes to the well-being of others, to their fulfillment as human
beings. Ethical principles, to be valid guides to morally right speech,
must be based on considerations of the effects of speech on every
side of man's nature that it touches.

It is helpful to think of the ethical requirements of speech communication as falling into two broad, but overlapping, categories: those
growing out of the area of formal public address, and those that arise
in the informal communications of group discussion and interpersonal
relations. The same basic values underlie each category, but they are
served in somewhat different ways.

One of the purposes of this book will be to urge that in public discourse, where relationships are relatively impersonal and the issues
public, the good is served by communications that preserve and
strengthen the processes of democracy, that provide adequate information, diversity of views, and knowledge of alternative choices and
their possible consequences. It is served by communications that
provide significant debate, applying rational thought to controversial
issues, recognizing at the same time the importance and relevance of
feeling and personal commitment. Further, the good is served by
communications that foster freedom of expression and constructive
criticism, that set an example of quality in speech content, in language use, and in fair play and civility.

---

[5] Melvin Rader, **Ethics and the Human Community** (New York: Holt, Rinehart and
Winston, 1965), p. 435.

In informal and interpersonal communications our values are served by speech that respects similar standards. But in interpersonal communication, where the impact of personality on personality is more direct and immediate, there are additional concerns. It is in such communications that we most fully share the human condition. The personality is served by speech which preserves the dignity and integrity of the individual ego, which makes possible the optimum sharing of thought and feeling, the experience of belonging and acceptance, and which fosters cooperation and mutual respect. If these aspects of interpersonal communication are not ordinarily thought of as having a significant ethical component, it is because we have lacked a sufficiently inclusive sense of moral obligation.

As we have noted, there is general agreement on our basic values and on our ethical principles when stated broadly. There is often disagreement on the application of general principles to specific actions. This is as it should be. We do not, and cannot, all see a situation from the same perspective. Moreover, the conditions of life are constantly changing, and values must be reinterpreted and principles adapted if they are to be applied constructively to new situations. Society receives its most important ethical dividends not from rigid ethical prescriptions, but from the struggles of men to reconcile their ethical conflicts. In this process light is shed on the different interests affected and their claims to consideration, and on the various factors that enter into each unique ethical problem. The resulting compromise is more likely to preserve the dignity and integrity of the individual than an arbitrarily applied moral prescription.

This book attempts to suggest what implications for speech communication follow from the basic concept of the good postulated. It attempts to state what it means for one's speaking to do justice to the concept of man as a being of dignity and intrinsic worth, with a capacity for rational choice. If at times the principles sound unrealistic or idealistic, let the reader ask himself whether he could ask less and still remain consistent in his conception of man. Let the reader ask whether other men's wants and needs are as legitimate as his own. If others have the same capacities, the same title to dignity, how else could one talk and still maintain one's integrity?

The philosopher Alfred North Whitehead once wrote: "The vigor of civilized societies is preserved by the widespread sense that high aims are worthwhile. Vigorous societies harbor a certain extravagance of objective, so that men wander beyond the safe provisions of personal gratification."[6]

Related readings

Articles

Chesebro, James W. "A Construct for Assessing Ethics in Communication," **Central States Speech Journal**, XX (Summer 1969), 104–114.

Haiman, Franklyn S. "A Re-Examination of the Ethics of Persuasion," **Central States Speech Journal**, III (March 1952), 4–9.

Levi, Albert W. "Language and Social Action," **Ethics**, LI (April 1941), 307–324.

Wallace, Karl. "An Ethical Basis of Communication," **The Speech Teacher**, IV (January 1955), 1–9.

Wieman, Henry N., and Otis M. Walter. "Toward an Analysis of Ethics for Rhetoric," **Quarterly Journal of Speech**, XLIII (October 1957), 266–270.

Books

Baier, Kurt. **The Moral Point of View: A Rational Basis of Ethics.** Ithaca: Cornell University Press, 1958.

Brandt, Richard B. "Toward a Credible Form of Utilitarianism," in **Morality and the Languages of Conduct**, eds. Hector-Neri Casteneder and George Nakhnikian. Detroit: Wayne State University Press, 1963. Pp. 107–143.

Fletcher, Joseph. **Situation Ethics.** Philadelphia: Westminster Press, 1966.

Garnett, A. Campbell. **Ethics: A Critical Introduction.** New York: Ronald Press, 1960.

Keller, Paul W., and Charles T. Brown. "An Interpersonal Ethnic for Communication," in **A Reader in Speech Communication**, ed. James W. Gibson. New York: McGraw-Hill, 1971. Pp. 43–49.

Maslow, Abraham H. **Toward a Psychology of Being.** Princeton, N.J.: Van Nostrand, 1962.

Smith, T. V., and William Debbins. **Constructive Ethics.** Englewood Cliffs, N.J.: Prentice-Hall (Spectrum Books), 1948.

[6] Alfred North Whitehead, **Adventures of Ideas** (New York: Macmillan, 1956), p. 371.

TWO

On telling the truth

When we make an ethical judgment about someone, one of our major questions concerns his truthfulness, his honesty. On the basis of everyday experience we recognize that people cannot get along together, carry on cooperative work, form associations and larger communities, unless they can rely on each other. Unless we can assume that people will do what they say they will do, that the information they give us will on the whole be accurate, we cannot carry on organized social life. Therefore, if we believe that the good is that which enlarges and enhances the human personality, and that the individual personality can only develop its potential as a participating member of a creative, cooperative community, then mutual dependability is essential to our realization of the good.

Since human interactions and transactions are carried on through communication, communications must be dependable—which is to say, truthful. Although we can all readily agree that truthfulness is important to morally right speech, we would probably find it difficult in many instances to agree on what being truthful means or entails. Most of us have been troubled at some time or other over the problem of whether we really know the truth or, knowing, whether we should tell it. Certain questions have occurred to all of us: Should we tell the truth even if it hurts someone? Need we go out of our way to tell the truth? Should we tell the truth about a fellow student's cheating on an exam, or a neighbor's income-tax evasion? Can we claim to be honest if we present only some of the facts about a situation? If we have a product to sell, are we morally obliged to tell about its weaknesses as well as its strengths? Is it all right to tell a lie to make someone feel better?

There are other questions which are not as likely to have occurred to everyone: How much information, and of what kinds, constitutes the truth in a given situation? Are our intentions or purposes part of the truth of something we say? Do we usually tell the truth about another person when we describe him or his behavior? If our listeners misinterpret our words, how much responsibility do we bear for the misconception they carry away with them? Does truthful speech imply any particular effort to avoid misunderstanding? Is there a difference between telling the truth and being honest? Is there such a thing as something being "true for me" but not for someone else?

Truth telling is plainly a complex matter, not only in the sense of deciding what is true, but in the sense of deciding whether the effects of telling it at a given time will be good or bad. We face some such decisions virtually every day. In this chapter we shall attempt some clarification of what truth telling entails, and our obligations toward it, given the concept of the good presented in the last chapter.

Truth telling, values, and language

In an essay entitled "On Telling the Truth," the Italian philosopher Benedetto Croce writes that "Falsehood enjoys the particular abhorrence of moralists, and it is in very truth more offensive than other forms of evil...."[1] Because falsehood is such a serious moral problem, he continues, it must be clearly understood. It is a mistake to define falsehood as a failure to tell the truth, because we have to admit that there are many instances in which the truth should not be told. There is the classic example "of the invalid who must be deceived as to his condition lest depression reduce his vital resources." In such instances, Croce says, our "conscience tells us that we are not really

[1] Benedetto Croce, **The Conduct of Life** (New York: Harcourt, Brace, 1924), p. 52.

lying." We are, in fact, doing our duty. There is also the case of the gossip, where the statements may be true, but may also be a "shocking offense against righteousness."

> When, then, should we tell the truth? And when should we not tell the truth? Just where does falsehood begin and end? Perhaps it would be better to preface these questions with another which is too often disregarded: what does it mean to tell the truth, to communicate the truth, that is, to others?
>
> If we think carefully, we see that once we have thought the truth we have already told it—to ourselves, that is, by virtue of the unity of thought and speech. But as for telling it aloud, as for communicating it to others—that is a serious matter, so serious that it is almost desperate. Truth is not a bundle that can be passed from hand to hand: it is thought itself in the actuality of thinking. How communicate that actuality to others?
>
> In fact, we never really communicate the truth. At best, when we address other people, we send out a series of stimuli we hope will move them into a state of mind identical with ours, so that they will think the truth that we are thinking. . . . We do not tell the truth because the most we can do is to send out sounds, which will in their turn provoke consequences quite beyond and apart from anything that is going on in ourselves.
>
> This puts a different face on the matter. The problem of communicating with others, of speaking to others, is no longer a problem of telling or not telling the truth, but of acting on others with a view to provoking certain actions in them. Among the many things required for this, truth-telling, which means truth-thinking, is one; but the overshadowing objective is that the life in people should be stimulated, changed, ennobled.[2]

In a sense, when we communicate we let loose words on others, accompanied, of course, by facial expression and other nonverbal cues. We may have a definite purpose in mind, to persuade, to clarify a point of view, or simply to state a fact, but our words do more. Our words, or the sounds we send out, "provoke consequences quite beyond and apart from anything that is going on in ourselves." Croce is concerned that people tell the truth, but he is more concerned about the total consequences of the communication than about the truth value

[2] **Ibid.,** pp. 54–55.

of some particular statement. It is, furthermore, not simply a matter of avoiding injury to someone, but that "the life in people should be stimulated, changed, ennobled."

Choosing such words and making such statements as will tell the truth that should be told present serious difficulties. When we are concerned about a direct relationship between a simple descriptive statement, such as "The ball is black," and the object it describes, there is, of course, no problem. But our communications are rarely so simple. The things we talk about, our relationships to these things, and our relationships to each other as human beings are usually complex, and the words we use mean different things to different people.

"Telling the truth," says the late German theologian Dietrich Bonhoeffer, ". . . is not solely a matter of moral character; it is also a matter of correct appreciation of real situations and of serious reflection upon them."[3] In his explanation of what is meant by telling the truth, Bonhoeffer says, in part:

> An individual utterance is always a part of a total reality which seeks expression in this utterance. If any utterance is to be truthful it must in each case be different according to whom I am addressing, who is questioning me, and what I am speaking about. The truthful word is not in itself constant; it is as much alive as life itself. If it is detached from life and from its reference to the concrete other man, if "the truth is told" without taking into account to whom it is addressed, then this truth has only the appearance of truth, but it lacks its essential character.[4]

An individual utterance is always a part of a total reality, a reality which includes not only all the related circumstances, but the purposes and values involved as well. The truth of discourse depends upon its being consistent with the purposes and values it presupposes, as well as appropriately related to the objective reality it represents. To use a simple example: If I refuse to transmit a bit of information about someone that could be derogatory (and from which no foreseeable good will come), I am being consistent with a belief in the desirability of privacy in personal life, and with a belief that the dignity and

---

[3] Dietrich Bonhoeffer, **Ethics**, ed. Eberhard Bethage, trans. Neville Horton Smith (London: SCM Press, 1955), p. 327.
[4] **Ibid.**, p. 328. Bonhoeffer's words are out of context here because of the theological cast of his thought, which is not revealed in this brief passage. The statement is highly relevant, however, without its theological interpretation.

integrity of the individual should be respected. In Bonhoeffer's terms, I am being true to a conception of man, to a set of values which is higher than that concerned solely with factual information. I am being more truthful. Thus, to be truthful in my utterances I must consider as much as I can of the relevant "total reality."

As Croce said, when we communicate we "send out sounds, which will in their turn provoke consequences quite beyond and apart from anything that is going on in ourselves." Our language, then, and our forms of expression are important to truth telling, and we need to be aware of how language and attendant meaningful cues function in communication. What Croce and Bonhoeffer would seem to be implying about language, the philosopher J. H. Randall, Jr., says explicitly in the following statements:

> The mechanisms of a language in the strict sense—the words, sentences, and bits of discourse formulated in accord with the vocabulary, grammar, and syntax of that language—do not reveal their powers of operating—what they can and cannot do, the "meanings" they can and cannot convey—apart from a determinate situation of communication.
>
> Thus a formal analysis of the inherent structure or "frame" of the specific mechanisms of language—bits of connected words and discourse—will reveal no determinate operation of these mechanisms, no definite "meaning" whatever. The operations of language—the "meaning" and "significance" communicated and received—belong not to those mechanisms, those "sentences" taken by themselves, but to the functioning of those mechanisms in the total linguistic situation, to the sentences as "used" in the particular context in which they are employed. If any of the factors in that context are altered—the occasion, the hearer, the attitude and intention of the speaker, his tone and inflection, etc.—the same connected words, the same "sentences," will convey a quite different meaning.[5]

More than this, language is so highly functional that the purposes of its users are an integral part of the total meaning. Randall says further:

> Ordinary language, in fact, is so practical in its genesis and character, so directed toward formulating the functional relations of means and ends, in terms of the activities and attributes of mechanisms or nouns, that it can never literally "describe" any encountered operations at all.

[5] John Herman Randall, Jr., "The Art of Language and the Linguistic Situation: A Naturalistic Analysis," **Journal of Philosophy**, LX (January 1963), 29–56.

It can express them only through formulating them in terms of the means-end powers of practically and emotionally significant agents or mechanisms. Thus we hear a bird singing. But we do not "describe" what we hear, the song itself: we say, "There's a wood thrush." Ordinary language is not representative or isomorphic in its structure, but "practical": to perform its functions, it has to reorganize natural structures into the activities of agents.[6]

The words of discourse, then, do not function in isolation, or with fixed meanings, or as direct representations of reality. Language when used in communication reflects and in a sense embodies the thoughts and feelings, the purposes and values of the persons using the language. As Croce says, when we are talking to people "we send out a series of stimuli we hope will move them into a state of mind identical with ours, so that they will think the truth that we are thinking. . . ." Indeed, all we can do is attempt to move others to experience or to share what we ourselves perceive, know, and feel.

The notion of truth telling is a complex and difficult one. We can speak of being truthful in various senses. Perhaps the most obvious is where someone makes a simple descriptive statement which can readily be verified—"The ball is black." Truthfulness here implies accuracy of description, the correspondence of the statement with a public reality. Where the descriptive statements are about a complex and changing phenomenon, they are potentially verifiable, but verification may be very difficult and for practical purposes never complete. Where the descriptive statement is about a private experience such as "I have a headache," verification may be impossible.

Most of our communications, however, have to do with more than description or representation; they involve human purposes and feelings: We seek to move our listeners, to influence them in thought and action. From this arises another sense of truthfulness, that which entails the speaker's revealing, or bringing his listeners to an awareness of, the feelings and intentions the speaker brings to the utterance (insofar as these are relevant to the listeners' purposes). Such awareness is necessary to the listeners' most informed and judicious response to the larger reality—the complex of meanings and purposes —of which the particular utterance is a part.

Further, since we all think and act on the basis of a set of values,

[6] **Ibid.**, 55–56.

usually unexpressed though none the less operative, it becomes a part of the truthfulness of a speaker whether he makes his listeners aware of the values that underlie his utterance, or that his utterance is designed to serve. This is of particular importance if the speaker's values differ from those his listeners assume underlie or are served by the communication.

The above aspects of truth telling are, of course, all involved to a greater or lesser degree almost every time we address another person. Before we discuss, in more practical day-to-day terms, these various modes of truthfulness, let us venture a general statement about the requirements of truth telling: If a speaker is to tell the truth, he must attempt to arouse in the mind of his listeners as clear, accurate, and complete a picture or conception of his subject as possible. Since he cannot say all there is to say about it, he must select certain parts or aspects to describe; the aspects must be those which are relevant for the listeners—that is, those which will provide the information needed for informed and constructive response. Moreover, since purposes, values, and feelings have much to do with the meanings the speaker intends and the listeners receive, the speaker must make clear his own values, purposes, and feelings, and adapt his discourse to compensate for the influence that the listeners' values and feelings will have on the meanings they discern in the words used. Again, the truth that needs to be told is determined by what the listeners need to know and feel in order to make the most informed, constructive response. At the level of human interaction truth and values are intertwined. The truth of discourse refers, not simply to empirically verifiable statements, but to a complex pattern of meanings relating a listener to some part of the world he experiences.

More briefly: Truth telling in communication implies the use of language in such a way as to arouse in the listeners as complete a concept as possible of the relevant aspects of whatever reality is being talked about, and whatever values, purposes, and feelings are relevant to the listeners' understanding of and most fully informed response to the communication.

Applications of the concept of truth telling

Application to various types of situations. In one sense of the word, "truth" is used to refer to a relationship of correspondence between a statement and that to which the statement refers, or which it describes or represents. A statement such as "A statue of George Washington is six blocks north and three blocks east of here," if accurate, has a relationship to the geography of the area that will evoke in the mind of a listener a concept of spatial relationships that will enable him to "know" where the statue is. The blocks may be longer than he thinks, the statue not as large as he anticipates, but if the spatial and structural relationships are accurate, that is all that is required for the statement to be true, in a simple and direct sense.

At this level we do not have much trouble with truth. The statement could, however, be misleading to a listener. If someone in a wheel chair, to whom distance poses a problem, were to ask about the location of the statue, it would be more true if, in addition to the accurate spatial relationships given, the information included the phrase, "The blocks are unusually long." The questioner might be assuming conventional blocks, and their unusual length would be highly relevant information. One might say, of course, that there are two questions involved: "Where is the statue?" and "How far away is it?" Two different answers are required to bring out the complete or needed information and either answer may be true. This is correct. The point being made here, however, is that that speech is most true which communicates the most accurate and complete conception of whatever is being talked about, the completeness depending upon what is relevant to the human needs and purposes involved. Such completeness not only makes the communication more true in the sense in which we are using the term, but more morally right in that the human personality addressed is more fully served.

To use a more complex illustration, let us consider the statement, "Juvenile delinquency is caused by emotional insecurity." If it is to make sense to say that this statement is true, the meaning of the terms must be clarified and shared, so that they can be related to that to which they purportedly refer. The words in this sentence are not as easily related to the reality to which they refer as the terms **north, block,** or **statue. Delinquent behavior** must be defined; the age levels for **juvenile** must be set; agreement must be reached on the symptoms of the feeling state called emotional insecurity, and on the relationship implied by the term **caused by.** In addition, data would be needed on the percentage of juveniles who, revealing the symptoms of emotional insecurity, are also engaged in or at some later time become engaged in delinquent behavior. Further, it would be important to have information on attendant circumstances which might reinforce or counteract the effects of emotional insecurity. And this would not be saying that there might not be other causes of juvenile delinquency.

Thus, in order to relate the statement "Juvenile delinquency is caused by emotional insecurity" to the state of affairs it describes, in order to determine whether the correspondence exists that enables us to say the statement is true, there must be a great deal of defining and qualifying of terms, and data consulted. It needs to be understood, too, that terms like **juvenile delinquency** refer not to the commission of some particular overt act as such, but rather to behavior that is not in accord with certain culturally accepted norms of behavior. **Delinquent** is an intellectual construct. A physical act has been reorganized into something which has a certain meaning relevant to human purposes and values. Truthful speaking about delinquency, and about similar subjects, demands that relevant meanings be made clear and that statements be consistent with the definitions agreed upon and with the assumptions underlying the definitions. We will return to this example later.

Let us take another example that presents additional problems. Suppose someone says, using the form of an ordinary factual statement, "Taxes are too high." We can reasonably assume when someone makes such a statement that he does not like the taxes he is paying and believes they should be lowered. Another person might, however, as legitimately say of the same taxes, "They are too low." It wouldn't make much sense to say that the original statement, "Taxes are too high," is or is not true. Ordinarily we speak of this as a value statement or judgment, one which expresses an attitude or belief. It may be true or false that someone holds this belief, but the belief itself cannot be so classified. If truth or falsity is to be involved, certain criteria must be set up against which the statement can be judged; there must be a state of affairs to which the statement corresponds. For instance, suppose criteria are established which are based on an analysis of the relationships among population, income level, taxation, production, and consumption. Assume that these criteria indicate that when taxes rise above a certain level relative to certain quantitative relationships among the factors mentioned, there is a decline in business activity. Then it could be said that "Taxes are such that a decline in business activity is imminent," and the statement would be true or false. If it was further postulated that a decline in economic activity is undesirable, or bad, and there is agreement on what is bad, then it could be said that "Taxes are too high," and in this context the statement could be thought of as true or false.

Thus far in the practical application of our concept of truth telling, we have only looked at descriptive, or purportedly descriptive, statements. Imagine now that you are listening to a speaker arguing against a particular tax bill, making much of the assertion that this bill would increase taxes which are already very high. Assume that he makes no false-to-fact statements and, indeed, makes such a good case for his proposition that you resolve to urge your congressman to vote against the measure. Now, suppose you learn that the speaker has large investments in an enterprise which will be affected by the tax bill in question, and you have reason to believe that his opposition stems mainly from his personal financial involvement. This puts his argument in a new light. His explicit statements, in a sense, are no less true, but you feel now that you understand more of the **truth of the situation.** More specifically, you probably feel that the speaker did not adequately reveal his purposes in speaking against the bill; you will probably feel you need additional information before you can decide for or against the bill; you may also feel that the speaker has treated you unfairly, not respecting fully your right as a human being to make up your mind on the basis of information available; you may feel you have been used.

It is apparent that the truth of a piece of discourse involves more than the truth of its individual descriptive statements. If the truth is to be told, statements must be made which give the listener an accurate conception of the state of affairs being discussed—that is, those aspects of the state of affairs which are relevant to the listeners. This plainly includes the motivations of the speaker.

Even what are ostensibly descriptive statements may involve purposes not immediately apparent. The statement "Juvenile delinquency is caused by emotional insecurity" may reflect the speaker's desire to cast doubt on the existence of other causes; it may be a defensive statement by which someone is seeking to explain away or excuse a delinquent act; it may be a statement designed to minimize the issue. Sometimes the context of the discourse enables the listener to perceive such latent meanings; at other times not. Here again we can see that the intentions associated with a statement may be a significant part of the truth of the situation which the listener needs to know in order to make the most intelligent response to the communication.

We have said that the truth of discourse is a function of its relationship to the values it presupposes, or to the value orientation of the listeners. An illustration of falsity in value relationships would be the case of a speech urging a policy that would ostensibly preserve certain values, but that would in actuality deny or restrict them. For example, suppose a speaker argues against certain minimum state requirements in educational standards. He might plead that such requirements will result in a loss of freedom for the schools, whereas local control will preserve their freedom. Now, it seems safe to say that control by a local school board is sometimes oppressive, restricting the school administration from developing more adequate curricula and hiring more capable teachers. This is freedom for the school board but hardly for the schools. The advocate in such a case may, of course, be sincere. Nevertheless, he appeals to his listeners in behalf of a widely shared value, the freedom of education, with which his proposal is essentially inconsistent. In fairness, we should admit that one might genuinely feel that control even by a shortsighted local board is, in the long run, a better safeguard for the freedom of education. And this might be the case. But if this is the point, it is precisely what should be made clear to the listeners if the speaker is to speak truthfully.

To use a further example, imagine that a representative of an association—professional, fraternal, political, or economic—speaks of the importance of preserving freedom and individualism. Certainly the extolling of the importance of freedom and individualism does not present a question of truth or falsity. If at the same time that the spokesman speaks, however, his association is lobbying for measures that will tend to restrict such freedoms, one must call into question the truth of the discourse. For instance, suppose the speaker is urging further restrictions on antitrust activity, enabling greater monopolization of business and industry. This would no doubt provide greater freedom for a small minority and less freedom of action for a larger majority. The restrictions on freedom of action for a significant number of people would be very relevant information for the listener who is to decide whether to support the measures in question. Such omission of relevant factors, in this case related to the actual operation of the values espoused, we have said is a failure to be truthful.

Further, apart from any specific issues being supported, the cere-
monial eulogizing of individuality and freedom may simply be designed to create a favorable public image of the association, with the
hope that the halo will carry over to various measures that the association seeks to have adopted. Without a knowledge of the association's
purposes, the listeners would not know the truth of the situation. The
speaker has spoken dishonestly because he has deliberately aroused
incomplete and inaccurate conceptions in the minds of his listeners.
It must be granted that the speaker may have a conception of freedom or individualism different from his listeners', and may not intend
deception. The speaker, however, has a moral obligation to make clear
his value assumptions, to relate them to the value expectations of his
listeners, and to make clear the purpose his speaking serves. These
are requisites of truth telling.

Related to the purposes and values reflected in speech are the
emotions aroused by the speaker; these too are relevant to the truth
of the discourse. Unless ideas are made interesting, listeners are
not likely to attend to the speaker. Usually the idea or purpose urged
must be shown to be vital to the lives of the listeners. It must
have a touch of excitement about it; it must have some "emotional appeal." Arousing the attention and appealing to emotions,
however, present serious problems of truth and ethics. The essential
problem is that of keeping the subject in appropriate emotional perspective. The communicator can create a false sense of urgency; he
can exaggerate the importance of the issue; he can arouse unwarranted hopes and fears, as well as false expectations. The most obvious examples of "emotional falsity" are found in the communications
of advertising. Through the total meaning generated by words and
visual associations, cosmetic ads, for example, imply a significance to
the life of the listener or viewer that is grossly exaggerated. At the
same time such advertisements imply a false sense of need, of urgency and expectation, related to the most vital needs for affection
and belonging. Such advertising is crassly dishonest, not in terms
of the actual or practical claims made, but in terms of the attempt to
relate the product advertised to the personality of the individual and
his or her social needs and desires.

Spokesmen for extremist groups are also often guilty of emotional
falsity. When terms like **communism** or **socialism,** or the more currently fashionable **fascists, pigs,** and **hippies,** are used again and again

with sinister connotations, yet without definition, these terms tend to gain a strong emotional charge that is associated, not with a specific meaning, but with the word. There is no meaningful correspondence between the discourse and what it describes, and the negative emotions become attached to various objects of dislike which have no relationship to any reasonably acceptable definition of the original term.

More common on the part of extremists are the excessive emotionality and the exaggerated fears which are generated, out of all proportion to any dangers upon which reasonable men could reasonably agree.

The truthfulness of more subtle expressions of value and emotion can perhaps be seen more clearly if the public communication is compared to a work of literary art. We may say of a novel that "it doesn't ring true." The values implied by the actions of the characters may not be consistent. The emotions expressed may not be in keeping with the characters themselves and their circumstances. Thus we sense a falsity in the characterization. We may not wish to call the author dishonest. We might speak of a lack of insight, of depth of understanding on the part of the author. We would still feel, however, that as a work of art the novel is not "true." Similarly, a speech may not ring true if the values expressed or implied are inconsistent with each other, or if the emotional tone is not consistent with the subject or with the speaker as a person.

There is thus a falsification of some aspect of the subject or speaker, and we are misled as to the nature of one or the other or both. As one writer puts it, "Art demands harmony, and indeed results from the fusion of personality and purpose."[7] As much can be said of speech, which partakes of the character of art. The fusion of personality and purpose is essential to a "true" work of communication.

We have spoken of discourse as being true to the degree to which the listener can achieve an accurate conception. Should we have said that the discourse is true to the degree to which it presents such an accurate conception? Can the speaker be responsible for all the possible misinterpretations a listener might make? Is he responsible if the listener gains a picture of the situation that the speaker did not intend? It seems plain that not all the responsibility can be placed on

[7] Albert Guérard, **Art for Art's Sake** (New York: Lothrop, Lee and Shepard, 1936), pp. 216–217.

the communicator. To suggest this fact, we have used the words "can achieve," not "does achieve." Misunderstanding is always possible; the adequacy of the discourse, its adaptation to the listener, has to be judged in the light of what can reasonably be expected of the communicator.

It is apparent that problems of truth telling become more complex as we move away from the level where truth is determined by an unambiguous correspondence between the words used and an objective reality to which they refer. From such a level of simple correspondence, through levels where the objective reality is complex and elusive, to levels where feelings, purposes, and values become an integral part of the total meaning to which expression is given, truth telling becomes progressively more difficult.

True discourse, or the truest discourse, as we have said, is that in which language is so used as to arouse in the listener as accurate a conception as possible of whatever part of reality is being represented, and of whatever purposes, feelings, and values are relevant to the listener's understanding of and most fully informed response to the communication. Every utterance expresses a part of a vastly larger whole of possible meaning. What is relevant from the larger whole of meaning depends upon several things: the needs, desires, and expectations of the auditors; the purposes and value assumptions of both speaker and listeners; the attitudes, needs and values of the larger community of which the speaker and listeners are a part; the alternatives open; the possible consequences of the various alternatives and the relationship of these consequences to the values of those concerned. The truth of discourse is always a matter of degree; there is no such thing as complete apprehension of the relevant information in a situation in which there is significant human interaction.

Qualifications and adaptations of discourse. Short of the privacy and purpose of the psychiatrist's office, it is absurd to speak of telling all, of being completely honest and candid in expressing one's thoughts and feelings. This is true in both private and public life. Common sense tells us as much. While there is great need for the proper kind of honesty and candor, there is also a need to recognize the circumstances under which the principles of truth telling need to be adapted to the circumstances of complex human relations. Croce placed the ennobling of the life in people above the factual truth of a statement in any given instance, if the two were in conflict. The adaptation of principle to circumstances is not the abrogation of principle, but its application so that the greater good is served in the long run.

When the President of the United States is engaged in delicate negotiations with the head of another state, it certainly may be in the interests of the citizens of both countries that certain information at his disposal become privileged—that is, not available to the general public. Even after the nature of the settlement is known, it may not be in the public interest that the details of the discussion be publicized. When our government plans alternative policies to deal with potentially aggressive foreign states, we do not expect the plans to be made widely known. In the difficult area of international policy we find it necessary to delegate power to an executive, and we do not demand, in the cause of honesty, that he divulge everything he knows and does. On the other hand, we must avoid the kind of secrecy that threatens the proper functioning of a democratic society. In a free society where people have the right to make choices—indeed, must make choices, at least of leaders and broad policy directions—the people must be informed. How much information about current negotiations and plans, and about immediate past negotiations that led to the present circumstances, should be made public is no doubt one of the most difficult questions facing leaders in a democratic society.[8] There are no easy answers. At the least, the question of public information should be under continuous study by a group of the most informed and responsible persons in our society, and the best decisions possible made from time to time. It would not seem wise to try to prescribe a rigid information policy for the future.

The problem of secrecy exists on the national level as well as on the international, on the individual as well as the organization level. We recognize the occasional need for executive sessions of congressional committees, for closed congressional hearings, and private labor-

[8] The seriousness of the ethical problem facing a public official with respect to what he should and should not divulge is suggested by a statement from Dag Hammarskjöld when he was Secretary General of the United Nations: "The most dangerous of all moral dilemmas: when we are obliged to conceal truth in order to help the truth to be victorious. If this should at any time become our duty in the role assigned us by fate, how straight must be our path at all times if we are not to perish." **Markings** (New York: Knopf, 1965), p. 147.

As this is being written, the so-called Pentagon Papers, having been turned over to the press by a former government official, point up the problem of public information in a most painful way. The legal and moral aspects of this disclosure will be the subject of discussion and debate for a long time to come.

management negotiations. We recognize the right of a company to withhold information about new products in the interest of legitimate competitive advantage, the privacy of certain legal proceedings, and the privileged nature of certain professional communications. We do not expect or want the doctor, priest, or minister to disclose what he learns about the people who go to him for help. In short, we realize that all human affairs simply cannot be conducted in public, so that we do not consider the withholding of information under certain circumstances as instances of dishonesty or as depriving others of their right to know. And the reasons are not difficult to see. Policies in stages of formulation might be seriously misunderstood by those not familiar with the problems being dealt with; contingencies need to be planned for, even though the chance of their occurrence might be very remote, and such planning (let us say for death or bankruptcy, natural disaster or war) could well be misinterpreted; isolated bits of information about a person or an organization, a misdeed or a misstatement, taken out of context could be misleading or damaging. Openness and candor for their own sake hardly seem justified, as when language which is offensive to some is used, and used where no redeeming social value seems to be served; or when intimate relationships are described where no purpose appears to be served but the desire or need to reveal one's own lack of inhibition, or moral superiority to a reserve which is looked upon as hypocrisy.

There are times, however, when the failure to make known certain public or private plans or actions, the failure to hold public hearings, the failure to publicize programs that affect the public interest, can be considered dishonest. The central question is whether the public interest will be best served, in the long run, by open or closed hearings; whether public participation in the particular discussion or decisions is provided by law or custom; and whether the part of the public affected can constructively participate in some other way. Traditional procedures have been guided, presumably, by such principles as fairness to all concerned, the maximum self-government consistent with national interest, optimum opportunity and protection for minority groups. These principles, however, have not always been fully translated into actual policy.

What passes for free and forthright reporting of events is often information deliberately selected and phrased: A type of news management is at work. A substantial part of what we call news about public and private agencies is in fact information released through public-information offices, which carefully select that which they want published. This procedure keeps much information from the citizens which they ought to have. Insofar as this is the case, the institutions concerned are not dealing honestly with the public. The argument may be made, of course, that some news management avoids certain dangers, such as the publication of haphazard and misleading information. Some selection of information to be released may be essential, but selection should be guided by the highest ethical principles and watched by a free and inquiring press.

The general problem of secrecy and management of information runs through the gamut of human affairs from the international level to the level of interpersonal relations. In interpersonal relations we must at times withhold our personal evaluations and certain kinds of information in order to preserve the dignity of our fellow human beings as well as to achieve harmonious relations with them.

There are other factors that need to be considered when we make judgments about the truthfulness of communications. In a given amount of time only a limited amount of information can be given. Selection of what is to be communicated is always operative, for we can never say all there is to be said about a situation. The shorter the time, the more vital selection becomes.

Another complex of factors concerns the audience itself. A speaker must consider his auditors' capacity for receiving and appreciating the material. There is no particular virtue in presenting ideas, facts, and figures to which an audience assigns no significance and which thus provide no basis for their intelligent making of choices. The time element, of course, enters in. If there is time to explain the material adequately, and the audience has the capacity to profit by the explanation, one is obliged to do so.

The institutional context in which the communicating takes place may provide extenuating circumstances. The lawyers for the prosecution and defense are not ordinarily expected to present the whole truth, but are expected to make as strong a case as possible for the side each represents. Trial procedure, which includes rules of evidence and discourse, rules relating to the examination and cross-examination of witnesses, impartial judging, and decision by a jury, is designed to maximize the possibility of a just choice between the alternatives of innocence and guilt. The system takes account of human imperfection in general and the motive of self-interest in particular, and seeks to counteract them. The unfortunate fact that an attorney may twist the meanings of the words he addresses to the jury, or attempt to confuse the witnesses, or appeal to emotions in a way calculated to circumvent the critical faculties of the jurors, cannot in any way be morally justified. Such procedures do not facilitate sound decisions; indeed, they militate against them. Such conduct on the part of lawyers is tolerated, not because it is desirable in itself, but because it is felt that the public interest, the cause of justice, is best served by the maximum of freedom of action for the lawyer within the given structure of rules prevailing in the court. The correctives in the system, including the opposing lawyer, are believed to be better insurance of just decisions than procedures too sharply delimited. We should not let trial abuses, however, provide norms for persuasion or ethical criteria for discourse. However, since those involved know the rules and procedures, we need to view legal pleading in context when making moral judgments about it.

When speaking takes place under known and accepted rules of procedure, such as formal debate, congressional hearings, and court trials, certain responsibilities for the presentation of information are compensated for by complementary sources of information and provision for immediate accountability. In some instances where each speaker is expected to make as strong a case as possible for one point of view, the juxtaposition of the arguments allows the listeners to make an informed, critical choice. In some instances the spokesman is only expected to answer questions put to him; the opportunity for interrogation opens the way for obtaining the information needed.[9] When, however, speaking does not take place under known and enforceable rules, when the individual speaker is not in a context that provides the correctives of complementary information or counterargument, then the responsibility to provide the information needed for choice making rests on the speaker. Under such circumstances truth telling—in the broad sense in which we are using the term—

[9] There is a very real question about the truth obtained through certain kinds of interrogations. The interrogating can confuse the witness and become threatening to such a degree that it is essentially coercive.

to the best of one's ability becomes a moral obligation. It is a moral obligation in every instance (given the qualifications discussed earlier)—the obligation is simply heightened; where the speaker is the sole source of information.

Obviously, the availability of information must be considered. No one expects a speaker to provide information that neither he nor anyone else can reasonably obtain. Too, the intentions of the speaker to tell the truth must be duly taken into account. Whether an act is morally right or wrong for the individual depends largely upon his disposition or intention. The act may not be good, in the sense of contributing to the well-being of people affected, but it is not morally wrong if the intention to do good is genuine. This statement needs qualification, of course. The speaker who seeks to influence attitudes and actions on matters of importance has the ethical obligation to inform himself as much as reasonably possible about the probable consequences of his proposal. It would be difficult indeed to suppose that a man had genuinely good intentions toward his listeners if he failed to anticipate the possible adverse effects of his acts.

Truthfulness and honesty. We have indicated that an act is good when it maximizes the experience of the good. We have said that an act is morally right when the doer tries to maximize the good and thoughtfully anticipates the consequences of his actions. We have recognized that it is possible to do something good without really intending to, in which case we can hardly call the act morally good. It is also possible to intend to do something good, only to have it turn out bad. We can still consider the action morally right, assuming that the speaker did his best to anticipate the consequences.

In a somewhat analogous sense, discourse can be said to be true if it maximizes the understanding and appreciation of the state of affairs with which it deals. A speaker is speaking honestly when he sincerely and thoughtfully intends to create in the minds of his listeners an accurate conception of the subject of his discourse and the relevant values and purposes, taking into consideration the many factors that may influence the meaning his listeners perceive. Of course, it is possible to express a truth inadvertently, but this can hardly be called honesty. One may also try to be truthful and yet not succeed in creating an accurate conception in the mind of the listener; this can still be called honest speech. Although we cannot hold the speaker totally responsible for the truth value of his discourse as his listeners perceive it, we can expect him to speak honestly to the best of his ability.

On trying to tell the truth

Croce's comment on the overshadowing objective of communication should by now have added meaning. The personality is the crux of the matter. If the good is that which enhances and enlarges the human personality and promotes well-being, then that should be said which in the long run best serves this purpose—that is, provides the bases for the optimum development and well-being of the personalities affected. We cannot, of course, always know whether what we say will serve this purpose; we can only make the best judgments of which we are capable, exercising the highest degree of imaginative insight and the most thoughtful anticipation of consequences. The position taken in this book is that truth telling as we have described it is crucially important to the communication that best serves the human personality.

A word of caution is necessary. We must be keenly aware that it may be dangerous to attempt to set ourselves up as judges of what is good and of what constitutes the truth that should be told in a given situation. There is danger that a particular political or religious creed or social theory may be assumed to embody **the** Truth, with the result that that which supports it is judged to be good, and that which opposes it is judged to be bad. To avoid this, there must be a commitment to objective appraisal of evidence and to the most rigorous reasoning of which we are capable.

Further, we must bear in mind that our use of language reflects our own conscious and unconscious purposes, and what we may think to be truth telling on our part may be more an attempt to satisfy our own needs than to communicate a truth to someone else.

In the last chapter the kind of speech that serves our values was briefly indicated. In interpersonal communication, we postulated, the personality is served by speech which preserves the dignity and integrity of the individual ego, which makes possible the optimum sharing of thought and feeling, the experience of acceptance and belonging, and which fosters cooperation and mutual respect. That should be said, then, which serves these ends. This includes truth telling. We should refrain from saying that which reduces well-being, that which works against these ends.

In public discourse the speech that serves our values, we have said, is that which strengthens the processes of democracy, fosters freedom of expression, provides information adequate for constructive decisions, engages in significant debate, examines alternatives and objectively appraises evidence and conclusions, and inspires to noble objectives. This includes truth telling.

As public problems become more complex, the choice of the information that should be presented becomes increasingly difficult, and so also does the problem of drawing the most warrantable conclusions. As the relevant data become more numerous and difficult to understand, more and more selectivity is essential and more careful reasoning is required. There is little doubt, however, that the more adequate and relevant the information, the better men can deal with their problems.

Not only is it difficult to know what constitutes the truth of a situation, but there inevitably will be disagreement about what the truth is. Where complex states of affairs are being described, there is not just one true description or one valid conclusion to be drawn. Especially important, therefore, to the achieving of social and political truth is the expression of many diverse views and interpretations. Equally important is confrontation of opinion with opinion, and critical examination and appraisal designed to put ideas to the test of soundness. Thus the interests of all concerned can be better known, the underlying values being served can be better clarified, and the alternative choices and their consequences more fully explored.

It should be plain that it is not possible to be explicitly prescriptive about what is the truth in or of a given situation. The truth of discourse is never absolute. Although we can only reach an approximation of the truth, this approximation should be as close as possible. Much is required of one who wishes to speak truthfully: good intentions; knowledge of facts, of values, purposes, and feelings; the ability to think critically and objectively. It requires something even more fundamental: a commitment to disinterested good will.

Throughout most, if not all, of the history of ethical thought, two cardinal principles have been postulated as underlying the morally good life: benevolence and justice. Benevolence is the will or inclination to do good, and justice implies impartiality and fairness.

We can know the good, but unless we have an inclination to do good, the knowledge is of little value. And there is no more fundamental ethical principle than impartiality; what we would will for others we must be prepared to will for ourselves. If we approach the problem of truth telling with benevolence and justice as our moral commitments, and then apply knowledge and reason to the best of our ability, we will begin to fulfill our obligations as human beings.

Related readings

Croce, Benedetto. **The Conduct of Life.** New York: Harcourt, Brace, 1924.

Day, Edmund E. **Education for Freedom and Responsibility.** Ithaca: Cornell University Press, 1952.

Mill, John Stuart. **On Liberty.** Chicago: Regnery (Gateway Books), 1955.

Ross, Murray G. "Ethical Goals of Modern Education," in **A Humane Society,** ed. Stuart Rosenberg. Toronto: University Press, 1962.

On significant choice

Significant choice and the ethics of speech

There can be little doubt that all of us accept a working belief in man's freedom of choice and his capacity to make rational decisions. We may feel that man's freedom of choice is always limited—limited by his natural capacities, his conditioning, and the alternatives open to him at any given time. We may feel that at best his decisions are only partly rational, yet it is this part that makes all the difference. It is a working belief in freedom and the possibility of rational choice that lies at the foundation of our system of political democracy with its provisions for the freedom we feel essential to the optimum development of the person. Our concept of the dignity of man is in large part based on and derived from our belief in the rationality of man. It is the rational autonomy of the individual that makes possible a sense of his dignity.

When we say, therefore, that those things are good which enhance and enlarge the human personality, we are saying that that is good which makes possible and contributes to the individual's making informed, independent, and critical choices that are meaningful in his life.

Philosophers of democracy have often spoken of the relation among freedom of choice, reason, and democracy. Charles Frankel speaks of the ideals of democracy as being the consent of the governed, the ideal of an open society, individual autonomy, and the ideal of responsible government.[1] Such ideals surely are without significant meaning apart from the possibility of rational decision and apart from a moral sense. Ralph Barton Perry says, ". . . freedom in relation to the social and physical environment means **effective choice.** Man is free, in other words, in proportion as he does or thinks as he chooses."[2] He relates choice to democracy by asserting that "at the root of modern democracy as built on the political principles of the seventeenth and eighteenth centuries, and embodied in the Declaration of Independence and the Federal Constitution, is the idea that the government of human affairs shall be vested in the reason of the individuals who live under it."[3]

The report of the President's Commission on National Goals emphasizes the possibilities for self-fulfillment, and the need for responsibility and self-discipline. "In freedom," states the report, "each thinker and doer has the right to self-expression in vocation and avocation. Liberty puts the maximum reliance upon self-discipline."[4] More directly to the point of this chapter, the report says: "The status of the individual must remain our primary concern. All our institutions— political, social, and economic—must further enhance the dignity of the citizen, promote the maximum development of his capabilities, stimulate their responsible exercise, and widen the range and effectiveness of opportunities for individual choice."[5]

One can hardly comment, however briefly, on the importance of choice in the life of the individual without recalling John Milton's famous **Areopagitica.** Milton was arguing in favor of freedom of publication and against the licensing laws of the England of his day. The state sought to allow the printing only of what it thought would meet the standards of virtue. Milton argued that the state, by making this decision for the people, would be undermining virtue itself. Virtue, he held, was not in unknowingly following the good and the true, but

[1] Charles Frankel, **The Democratic Prospect** (New York: Harper & Row [Colophon Books], 1962), pp. 33–39.
[2] Ralph Barton Perry, **The Humanity of Man** (New York: George Braziller, 1956), p. 110.
[3] **Ibid.,** p. 97.
[4] Henry W. Wriston, "The Individual," in **Goals for Americans** (Englewood Cliffs, N.J.: Prentice-Hall [Spectrum Books], 1960), p. 53.
[5] **Goals for Americans,** p. 3.

rather in knowing both good and bad, true and false, and deliberately choosing the good and the true. Virtue, he insisted, was in making the right choice, not in the conduct itself.

The relationship of free, informed, and critical choice to the ethical aspect of speech should be plain, as should our moral obligation. When we influence others to act, we bear some responsibility for the consequences of their action. Such influence occurs, and most obviously, when we urge someone or a group of listeners to accept a point of view or adopt a specific course of action, but it also occurs in many day-to-day, informal communications where we may move family, friends, or co-workers to attitudes or action. There is, however, a yet more important moral obligation, if we assume that men should be self-determining as far as possible, making free and informed choices as to the actions they will take. The moral rightness of our speech then turns in large part on the kind of choice making our speech fosters. It must be emphasized that here we are primarily concerned, not with the end result of the choosing (such as the election of a political candidate), but with the attitudes and judgmental processes that lead to the decision. This is a concern about preserving and developing the independence and autonomy of the person, the voluntary and informed nature of the choices he makes. In yet other words, we are concerned whether the choice-making process we encourage, directly or indirectly, is consistent with the self-fulfillment of the personality we are touching. We might, for instance, urge someone to the doing of an ethically good act, but we might through our way of urging be fostering uncritical, overemotional decision making, the kind of decision making that would be inconsistent with a self-determining personality.

What kind of choice making is most consistent with our dignity as human beings, and hence does justice to our moral nature? Given the values subscribed to here, it is choice making that is voluntary, free from physical or mental coercion. It is choice based on the best information available when the decision must be made. It includes knowledge of various alternatives and the possible long- and short-term consequences of each. It includes awareness of the motivations of those who want to influence, the values they serve, the goals they seek. Voluntary choice also means an awareness of the forces operating within ourselves.

We recognize, of course, that what we are talking about is a matter of degree. Realizing that we have to make decisions without adequate information, what we seek is simply the best information possible under the circumstances. We realize, too, that there is no such thing as complete freedom of choice; we are always under various kinds of pressures to do one thing or another. What we seek is the maximum freedom of choice possible in any given case.

If we feel that such decision making is most consistent with our own human dignity, with our nature as autonomous personalities, then it is the kind of decision making we must seek for others, else we violate the fundamental ethical principle of reciprocity. The position taken in this book is this: When we communicate to influence the attitudes, beliefs, and actions of others, **the ethical touchstone is the degree of free, informed, and critical choice on matters of significance in their lives that is fostered by our speaking.** We shall call this **significant choice.**

The criterion of significant choice

Making the opportunity for significant choice on the part of the listener an ethical criterion for the speaker presents several problems; it is not a simple measure of morality. The meaning and applications of the concept of significant choice can perhaps best be made clear by a discussion of some of the problems it entails as well as the communicative acts it implies.

All persuasion may appear to be immoral. If the listener should be given the maximum opportunity for significant choice, is it not then wrong to attempt to influence that choice? As intended here, this is emphatically not the case. What it does mean is that the listener's decision should be a free and responsible decision—free and responsible because of the knowledge of alternatives and their consequences, and of the interests and pressures operative in the situation. The speaker may well urge a particular choice among the alternatives made known. However, if the speaker respects the integrity of his listener, he will not want his listener to accept a point of view that the latter has not himself been able to reach by thoughtful assessment of the relevant information. This is respect for the integrity of the person, and is central to our ethical concept.

The listener often cannot make the choice. This objection says that there are many situations in which the listener cannot possibly make a constructive decision on his own. Here, as with all general principles, there are built-in qualifications. When we lay down the principle that men should have the opportunity for self-determination, we obviously assume a capacity for intelligent judgment. Similarly, when we say the individual should have the opportunity for self-determining choice, we mean that, given the circumstances, it is possible for him to make a significant choice. It may be that the individual is in no position to make a choice based on assessment of relevant information. In a complex society there is a great deal of diversity in the responsibilities assumed and the functions performed by various individuals. Of necessity there is much delegation of authority and decision making, in both the private and the public sector. No one should be expected or urged to make decisions outside the area of his competence and responsibility. Obviously the layman cannot make decisions that demand the specialized knowledge of the expert, whether it be in the field of medicine, law, architecture, tax policy, or what have you. The individual worker cannot very well decide company policy, the individual soldier decide strategy, the individual citizen prescribe taxes—not only for lack of information and training, but because the coordination of large and complex aggregates of men and materials requires a certain amount of centralized planning and authority. Not only where specialized or social problems are involved, but where the individual's immediate life is concerned, his choice making is often restricted: If he is unemployed he may choose to work, but a job may not be available; he may want to choose a different job, but his skills limit him; he may want to choose to develop certain skills, but he may not have the money to do so; he may lack needed talent; he may lack required physical capacities; and so on. Indeed, the individual may even choose not to be depressed, but may not be able to shake his depression. Such obvious limitations on the individual's choice making do not negate the fact that there are innumerable human situations in which he can and does choose: He chooses what he will think and say, and much of what he will do and how well he will do it; he chooses his political party and candidates, and can choose to persuade others; he chooses his church, his associates, much of his orientation toward life, and so on and on. What we are saying is simply that as a general ethical principle communications should maximize, or perhaps better "optimize," the opportunity for significant choice. The fact that at times such choice may not be possible or may be severely restricted, or that even at times it might not be wise to attempt to encourage reflective choice—as when there is no time and action is urgent—does not invalidate the general ethical principle. When we let one value take precedence over another at some particular time, we are not abandoning the latter, but trying to serve the higher value. If we tell a lie to save someone from anguish or to save a life, by that act we do not condone lying but feel that the principle of saving a life or of being kind takes precedence at times over the principle that we should not tell lies.

Exceptional circumstances, then, do not invalidate the principle that places free, informed, critical choice at the center of our ethical concerns, and they do not set the tone or provide the criterion for ethical judgments about our day-to-day informal and formal speaking.

People do not behave rationally. There is another objection, which is more subtle and perhaps more troublesome—namely, that in actual practice people often do not, even though given the opportunity, make up their minds on the basis of a rational consideration of the available information. Experiments in which short speeches are used to change the attitudes of an audience are frustratingly inconclusive as far as concerns revealing with any consistency which kinds of material, organization, or presentation are most influential in bringing about attitude change.[6] So-called logical appeals—that is, arguments based on appropriate evidence and reasoning—are apparently no more effective in changing attitudes than are "emotional" appeals (persuasion based on appeals to feelings or emotions), except perhaps with particularly sophisticated audiences. Studies utilizing the "congruity principle" reveal that when a speaker is attempting to influence the attitude of his audience toward a proposition, three of the most significant factors, or variables, are (1) existing attitudes toward the speaker, (2) existing attitudes toward the proposition, and (3) whether the speaker supports or opposes the proposition.[7] Not the content of the speech or the presentation as much as the existing pattern of at-

---

[6] See, for example, Carl I. Hovland, Irving L. Janis, and Harold H. Kelley, **Communication and Persuasion** (New Haven: Yale University Press, 1952); and H. I. Abelson, **Persuasion: How Opinions and Attitudes Are Changed** (New York: Springer, 1959).
[7] See, for example, David K. Berlo and Halbert E. Gulley, "Some Determinants of the Effect of Oral Communication in Producing Attitude Change and Learning," **Speech Monographs**, XXIV (March 1957), 10–20; and Charles E. Osgood, George J. Suci, and Percy H. Tannenbaum, **The Measurement of Meaning** (Urbana: University of Illinois Press, 1957), especially pp. 199 ff.

titudes and the tensions created in the minds of the listeners by conflicting attitudes seem to be most influential in attitude change. When
people encounter a significant new idea that conflicts with their existing pattern of beliefs and attitudes, they feel uncomfortable; tension
is created. They will move to reduce the tension by changing their
original attitudes, by rejecting the new idea, or by adapting the idea
to fit the original attitudes—all examples of the congruity principle in
operation. The acceptance or rejection of the idea appears to bear
little relationship to the nature of the argument **per se** used for or
against it.

Further, the influences which do bring about attitude change would
seem to give additional credence to the view that people frequently
do not come to attitude change as a result of critical evaluation of
alternatives. James A. C. Brown states, "One of the most successful
means used today to bring about attitude change is the creation of a
group in which the members feel belongingness since in these circumstances the individual accepts the new system of values and beliefs
by accepting belongingness to the group."[8] Speaking of the mass
media he says that "clearly **suggestion** is one of the main weapons of
the propagandist and the commercial advertiser."[9] In elaborating on
propaganda he adds, "All propaganda messages tend to occur in three
stages: the stage of drawing attention and arousing interest, the stage
of emotional stimulation, and the stage of showing how the tension
thus created can be relieved (i.e., by accepting the speaker's
advice)."[10]

We need not belabor the point. But if experimenters find, in experimental situations, that "logical" appeals or arguments are no more
effective in changing attitudes than are nonlogical appeals, and if
commercial and political persuaders find that they are more successful when they bypass the listeners' critical faculties, is the view still
tenable that we ought to try to foster informed, critical choice when
urging changes of attitude? In reply we must recognize that the
propagandist and commercial advertiser do not have as their primary
interest the developing of informed, critical, self-determining personalities. Their primary interest is in influencing their audiences to
some overt action, predetermined by the persuader. The way in which

[8] James A. C. Brown, **Techniques of Persuasion** (Baltimore: Penguin, 1963), p. 67.
[9] **Ibid.,** p. 75.
[10] **Ibid.,** p. 77.

propagandists and advertisers expressly avoid presenting relevant information and a critical discussion of alternatives reveals that they do feel that these may stimulate independence of action; they fear that informed, critical examination of the issues will stand in the way of their manipulation of the audience. Reflective, independent thought seems to be the last thing the professional campaign manager wants. Information and logical argument are not good manipulating techniques, but they are significant in evoking genuinely voluntary choice. The main question is, What kind of choice making do we want?—which is to say, What kind of people do we want? It depends upon what we value.

It might be tempting for someone to refer to the experimental evidence, and then to say that because experiments do not reveal that logical argument is more effective in changing attitudes than nonlogical persuasion, it follows that people are not really logical. They do not really make rational decisions, and therefore we have no obligation to urge them to do so. An interesting fact about experiments is that the experimenters must be very careful to control the variables in the experimental situation if their results are to be reliable. If the subjects in the experiment are aware of what is going on, the results may no longer be of value. In other words, human beings have the capacity to learn; they have the capacity to reflect on what is happening to them and to change their responses. If they think, for example, they are being manipulated, they may become angry and turn against the manipulator. Thus, when in an experiment it is determined that under the given circumstances people respond in a particular way to a particular set of stimuli, what the experiment reveals is that the given group of subjects, at its present level of learning, in its present state of conditioning, tends to respond in a given way. Provided with some additional knowledge, many of them will not respond that way again under the same circumstances. This we assume, of course, when we try to educate people. In fact, we might say that the educational process or the learning process is one of widening the range of effective responses open to the individual. Among the things that people can and do learn is to respond more reflectively and critically to persuasive messages. That such learning seems to be a slow process and perhaps hardly occurs at all in some does not mean that a significantly greater proportion of people could not learn to respond more independently, thoughtfully, and objectively than they have done heretofore.

People do not care about being rational—why push them? The point may still be made: If people are not inclined to make up their minds on the basis of the evidence available and reasoned consideration of alternatives, what obligation have we as speakers to try to influence them to do differently? If people do not seem to care about informed, critical choices, why should the speaker feel responsible for trying to foster them? These questions stem from a failure to appreciate the importance of choice making to the preservation of our basic values. Certainly most all of us feel some inclination or obligation to do what we understand as the right thing. We realize that unless most people feel this way, a free society cannot exist. We would not urge our fellow citizens to vote for a man whose actions we feel would be destructive of our values; we would have a guilty conscience if we lied outright about a candidate; we would think it wrong to damage another's reputation in order to gain an advantage for ourselves. In other words, we have a strong feeling about working for good ends, as we see them, and avoiding bad ones. What we have failed to appreciate is that the practice of highly emotionalized, uninformed, and uncritical choice making is, in the long run, destructive of our individual and social values. A free, democratic society depends upon citizens who choose responsibly, who recognize manipulative methods and extremist appeals, and who look for relevant evidence and warrantable conclusions.

Moreover, even though men often may not make "rational" decisions, if we feel we have a moral right to influence their decisions we surely incur a moral obligation to consider both the consequences of such choices and the choice-making procedure. We incur an obligation to try to bring about the kind of decision making that best serves the moral nature of men and the processes of democracy. In a democracy, for example, the kind of candidate men choose to support for public office is important, but how they choose him, how they go about making up their minds about him, is of yet greater importance. The kind of decision making engaged in will ultimately determine the kind of leadership a society has and the strength of its institutions. The objectivity, the informed and critical nature of the individual citizen's choice, may be limited, but whatever we can do to help promote such qualities of thought, in such proportion will we preserve the basic values of our society.

It is instructive to remind ourselves that the professional persuaders, who realize that the public at large does not always behave rationally, try themselves to arrive rationally at the persuasive techniques they employ on the "nonrational" citizen. The advertiser who sells soap or cars carefully and objectively analyzes the "public" taste, its whims and fancies, its buying habits, and carefully tailors his advertising to appeal to these whims and fancies. Similar techniques are used in political campaigns. The campaign manager uses his rational capacities to the utmost to devise means of influencing voter choice, usually on methods for influencing that choice without stirring up critical thought. It seems safe to say that if as much ingenuity were used to arouse a desire for, and to develop the ability to make, informed and critical choices among candidates and policies as is used to arouse impulsive choices, the degree of rationality in political decision making on the part of the citizenry could be appreciably increased.

There is, of course, no such thing as complete objectivity or a "public interest" apart from individual interests. The public interest is made up of individual interests, and a democratically arrived-at policy is one that is a compromise among the many interests represented and that accomplishes the best possible under existing circumstances. What we are interested in is not a fixed set of rational criteria, but the thoughtful assessment of alternatives, the long view rather than the short view, future interests as well as immediate interests, the greatest good for the greatest number rather than undue privilege for particularly aggressive minorities. The average citizen is certainly capable of becoming more impartial and critical in coming to his decisions if he is encouraged to do so by the makers of public opinion.

The question raised above—if people are not inclined to make up their minds on the basis of rational and impartial considerations, what obligation do we have to try to influence them to do so?—has further implications. It is of the essence of ethical principles that they do not simply reflect what people happen to be in the habit of doing at a particular time. If ethical principles do not transcend everyday behavior—that is, if they do not state what **ought** to be done rather than reflect what is being done—they are no longer ethical principles. It is precisely because they express an overriding **ought** that they can be general guides to behavior. For example, we do not think racial discrimination is justified because it has become part of the habit pattern of a community to discriminate against certain of its members because of their color. On the contrary, we feel we have a duty to urge the members of the community not to discrim- inate. The principle of equality transcends for us whatever inequalities may exist in particular communities.

That most people may not approach problems of public concern with the intention of making informed and impartial judgments is no reason why we should not try to influence them to do so. If we believe that men would in the long run make wiser, morally better decisions if they were to enlarge the component of rationality in their thinking, then we have an obligation not only to attempt to create the conditions that will make such rationality possible, but also to encourage it.

Significant choice and the marketplace of ideas

It is impossible for any one speaker to provide all the necessary information and knowledge of alternatives and possible conse- quences that would permit the opportunity for optimum choice making. The individual's knowledge is necessarily limited, and his view inevitably biased. The solution to this problem, it seems to be generally felt, lies not in expecting the individual speaker to be more objective and informative, but in having many different speakers present their conceptions of the issues under consideration, thus providing adequate information for intelligent decision making. John Stuart Mill in his essay **On Liberty** went so far as to say that the only way to do justice to an argument is to hear it from a person who actually believes it and who defends it in earnest.[11]

The point, well taken, is an important democratic principle: If there is free and unhampered expression of opinions, the many com- peting interests, by presenting their respective views and arguments

[11] John Stuart Mill, **On Liberty** (Chicago: Regnery [Gateway Books], 1955), pp. 52–53.

and criticizing others, will provide the kind of information and critical appraisal that will make possible for the listeners the most constructive choices. This "marketplace of ideas" is fundamental to a democratic society.

Within our strong tradition of public discussion of controversial issues, of reliance on the test of the marketplace, there has, however, developed an unfortunate lack of individual responsibility for what is said. Men appear to assume that the opportunity for discussion and rebuttal absolves them of the responsibility for the adequacy of information they present, and even for the truth of what they say. They seem to feel that the test of the marketplace permits any extreme of bias and self-interest, any extreme of persuasive technique.

Such lack of individual responsibility is dangerous to the democratic process, to the very freedom that makes public discussion possible. The strength of our democracy attests to the amount of irresponsiblity it can absorb; nonetheless, it takes little imagination to see the possibilities for more constructive choices if each advocate felt individually responsible for the adequacy of the information he presents.

There are limits to what can be expected of an individual speaker. If he has conscientiously informed himself, if he discusses the issues honestly and objectively, with a commitment to his listener's right to know and choose, we can ask no more. At the same time, a free society can ask no less. The responsible presentation and discussion of diverse views permits and fosters the kind of choice making that is the essence of a free society. "Freedom as a social ideal or standard," writes Perry, "refers to the enlargement of this freedom for effective choice."[12] Freedom is proportional to the opportunity for significant choice. In Perry's words, "Whatever determines what alternatives shall be made known to a man controls what the man shall chose **from.** He is deprived of freedom in proportion as he is denied access to **any** ideas or is confined to any range of ideas short of the totality of relevant possibilities."[13]

No one, of course, can know of all the relevant possibilities; freedom is never absolute. Our effort must be to make this "freedom of effective choice" as great as possible.

[12] Perry, **The Humanity of Man,** p. 105.
[13] **Ibid.,** p. 110.

Motivation to significant choice

The speaking we believe to be most morally right is that which con-tributes most to the possibility that the listener can make free, in-formed, and critical choices. Now we will add: **and which motivates the listener to such choices.**

The latter is an aspect of persuasion that has been almost com-pletely neglected. We hear much about our ethical responsibility for motivating listeners to socially constructive choices (to ethically good choices insofar as we can judge this), but little about our ethical obligation to motivate listeners to the kind of choice-making methods most likely to achieve constructive, ethically good decisions. If we feel that people should be motivated to socially good choices, it is just as reasonable to say that they should be motivated to socially good choice-making procedures. In fact, it is strangely inconsistent to urge people to morally right action without at the same time urging them to the kind of thought processes most likely to result in such action. The former our political and religious leaders often urge; the latter rarely. It is as if leaders wanted to reserve the right to make the choices of their listeners. We do expect them to use their special knowledge and experience to point the way as best they can, but not at the expense of our opportunity for self-determining choice. This negates the autonomous and moral nature of the action for us.

And so too, of course, when we ourselves seek to influence others. If we seek to move our listeners to choose some course of action, not only do we incur a moral obligation with respect to the ethical nature of the end result of that action, but with respect to the kind of choos-ing we encourage. And since making choices among acts is a lifelong process, the quality of the choosing is without doubt the more impor-tant ethical issue.

Self-understanding and significant choice

This chapter began with the assumption that free, rational choice is to a meaningful degree possible. Indeed, we indicated that such freedom and rationality are basic to the notion of the dignity of man and to the concept of a democratic society. We realize at the same time, however, that what we think of as free, rational choice may be less free and less rational at a given time than we actually feel it to be, and this gives rise to a question about the kind of responsibility we may have for understanding our own motivations. As one writer says, ". . . ethics involves understanding of self because ethics assumes or calls for rational choice and behaviour by relatively mature individuals. And such behaviour is not possible for those who are unaware that the goals they pursue are selected for reasons quite different from the reasons they suppose."[14] And further, "Understanding of human behaviour, and especially of one's own behaviour, is difficult indeed. But surely if our actions are to be ethical, we must make the effort to understand the forces which seem to push us in one direction or another. To be ethical requires . . . that we be rational—and to be rational requires understanding of man in general, and of self in particular."[15]

In a previous chapter it was stated that the intentions of the doer are an important part of the moral quality of his acts. We pointed out, however, that the individual is obligated to give careful thought to the possible consequences of his actions, else his good intentions are ethically meaningless. We must now add that, as suggested above, the individual must also give careful consideration to his own motivations. In a sense we have taken this into consideration before in that we have spoken of the importance of objectivity and impartiality in ethical decisions. These are the qualities that remove our judgments from the special biases and interests that are a part of all of us. But it is some understanding of our own motives, needs, interests, attitudes, conflicts, and frustrations that make objectivity possible, and to an extent impartiality as well, although the latter is largely a result of a basic disposition to disinterested good will. If we have some understanding of why we feel as strongly as we do about certain issues (because, say, of childhood conditioning, our group relationships, economic involvement, or some special need), we can put our own feelings into better perspective and more fully appreciate the attitudes of others. We can be more aware of our own predilection to see and select some facts rather than others, to feel anxiety or resentment toward some ideas, to favor certain personalities rather than others. If we are truly to respect the integrity of our listeners we must do our utmost

[14] Murray G. Ross, "Ethical Goals of Modern Education," in **A Humane Society,** ed. Stuart Rosenberg (Toronto: University of Toronto Press, 1962), p. 32.
[15] **Ibid.,** p. 33.

to understand and compensate for the biases that otherwise might cause us unconsciously to prejudge an issue. If, through our communications, we are to enlarge the opportunities for free choice on the part of our listeners—both by precept and example—we need a freedom of mind ourselves, a hospitality to the new and different, which permits our reasoning selves to consider alternative choices. Such qualities of mind depend in no small degree on a knowledge of ourselves. Surely such self-knowledge will help us better to understand and appreciate the possible motivations of our listeners, and the different perspectives from which they may see the world, permitting us to adapt our communications to them more adequately.

Emotion and significant choice

The emphasis on rationality that has pervaded this chapter does not imply any attempt to eliminate the emotional component in human thought and action. On the contrary, we recognize that the emotional components of interest, hope, excitement, aspiration, love, hate, anxiety, imaginative sympathy, and faith are an integral part of human experience. In fact, action on any proposal would necessitate the motivation of emotional involvement and commitment. It is hatred of a wrong, love of a right, concern for neighbor, self-interest, that move men to act. Without such feelings men would be apathetic and purposeless. A part of the problem of motivating an audience to informed, self-determining choice is the problem of evoking the appropriate emotions. An idea is not fully understood or appreciated unless men's feelings about the idea are understood. Men, institutions, movements, societies, cultures, cannot be understood and appreciated apart from the range of human feeling with which they are imbued. One may, for example, read the description of a church building and read about the church program, and yet understand little of the significance of the institution without some appreciation of the personal commitment it represents and the feelings it arouses because of the faith and hope it symbolizes. The understanding of an idea is simply not complete apart from an appreciation of the feeling it inspires.

There is in our society today a renewed appreciation of the place of feeling and emotion in human life. There has been an emotional austerity in much of our culture which we realize has left us unfulfilled. In our schools and colleges there has been an unbalanced emphasis on logical rigor or scientific method in human thought that has too often relegated consideration of human values, the cultivation of spiritual and esthetic experience, to the perimeter of academic concerns. There has been, not too much science, but too little poetry, and a failure to understand the most appropriate roles for both in human culture.

The reaction we have seen against "arid intellectualism" has its own dangers, however. We may not have solved our social problems through reason, but we must also realize that we will most assuredly never solve them without the use of reason. Dealing with our grievous social ills is not simply a moral but a mental task. For example, to provide food and clothing for the destitute people of a hungry world it is not enough to feel great compassion for their plight. Our scientific and technological resources must be mobilized and directed toward the task. Growing food in a commune garden and hand-weaving cloth, though laudable pursuits, will not suffice.

The problem then, is not to dissociate emotion from reason, but to arouse appropriate emotion and integrate it with reason. Love and compassion are needed to motivate people to help others, but a vague, generalized love of mankind does not help much unless it is accompanied by thoughtful consideration that focuses on real people and their specific needs, and the best reasoning is used to design specific measures to help them. Hatred too has its place. But a general hatred of vague, undifferentiated wrongs does not lead to corrective action; more likely it will lead to a corresponding general fear and resentment that itself leads to blind or ill-considered action. General hatred cripples the critical faculties, destroys imaginative sympathy, and tends to provoke destructive action. It is hatred of wrong accompanied by reasoned analysis that permits focusing on specific problems and their causes. Commitment to the good is essential, but rational analysis and action are needed for its realization.

Our communications should be aimed toward bringing about a constructive balance between thought and feeling in the self-determining choices we encourage. Objective, rational thought is not enough; it must be coupled with imaginative concern for, and a moral commitment to, our fellowmen. As A. E. Morgan puts it, "We have here, then, the two inseparable principles of a good society—a free, critical, objective inquiry, given effectiveness by ethical commitment;

and powerful ethical motive given direction and enlightenment by critical objective inquiry."[16] His statement quoted in the preface which
elaborates on these principles is well worth repeating:

> We must have free, critical, objective inquiry, without boundaries or
> precommitment or qualification—though not without humility and a
> sense of proportion; and we must have passionate, whole-hearted com-
> mitment to the best we know, again with humility and a sense of propor-
> tion. Too often we have thought of critical inquiry and moral enthusiasm
> as mutually exclusive. Only to the extent that they are organically united
> do we have the conditions essential for the preservation of democracy
> and freedom.[17]

Related readings

Hocking, William E. **Freedom of the Press.** Chicago: University of Chicago
Press, 1947.

Meiklejohn, Alexander. **Free Speech and Its Relation to Self-Government.**
New York: Harper, 1948.

Mumford, Lewis. **The Conduct of Life.** New York: Harcourt, Brace, 1951.

Nilsen, Thomas R. "The Ethics of Persuasion and the Market Place of Ideas
Concept," in **The Ethics of Controversy: Politics and Protest,** eds. Donn
W. Parson and Wil A. Linkugel. Proceedings of the First Annual Sym-
posium on Issues in Public Communication held at the University of
Kansas, June 27–28, 1968.

Nixon, Charles R. "Vital Issues in Free Speech," **Ethics,** LXII (January 1952),
101–121.

[16] A. E. Morgan, "Ethics and the Functioning of Democracy," in **The Scientific
Spirit and Democratic Faith;** papers from the Conference on the Scientific Spirit
and Democratic Faith, New York, May 1943 (New York: King's Crown Press, 1944),
pp. 26–27.
[17] **Ibid.,** p. 26.

FOUR

On persuasion

Almost everything we say or do in our interactions with others has some effect—sometimes slight, sometimes serious. While some of the effects may be brought about unintentionally, for the most part in such interactions we are seeking to influence attitudes and behavior, to win favorable, supporting responses from others. As our efforts to influence our fellow human beings become more deliberate and directed toward more specific ends—and the more so if the ends are public—we term the effort persuasion.

Persuasion, whether directed to one person or a thousand, implies that those to be influenced have a choice. Since a democratic society is predicated on the right of each citizen to choose freely among alternatives open to him in both private and public life, persuasion plays a vital role. Men choose (within limits, of course) their work, their homes, and their social, religious, and political affiliations, and express their preference for leaders and laws. Given the great diversity of interests among men, much persuasion is required for the establishment of common goals and a community of effort toward their achievement. Men must be persuaded to cooperate in community projects, to support organizations vital to society, such as unions, churches, public service agencies, professional groups, and political parties, and to support policies from the local to the national level. Persuasion to such action rather than coercion is the way of a democratic society, and we believe this is consistent with the dignity of the human personality. As Yves Simon puts it:

> Roughly a man is subjected to coercion when power originating outside himself causes him to act or be acted upon against his inclination. . . . Persuasion, on the other hand, is a moral process. To persuade a man is to awaken in him a voluntary inclination toward certain courses of action. Coercion conflicts with free choice; persuasion implies the operation of free choice.[1]

Insofar as we think of the principle of persuasion and its function in a democratic society, we find it ethically desirable. Something seems to happen, however, when the principle is applied in the practical affairs of men. Persuasion as it occurs in propaganda, lobbying, political campaigning, sales promotion, and so forth, often violates the ethical principles presented in the previous chapters. It is as if persuasion as an idea or principle tends to become corrupted when translated into action. This should not surprise us, however. Where self-interest can be served through persuading others to action, the temptation can be strong to serve that interest by using whatever means or techniques are available. And in a free society the opportunities are many.

It is the purpose of this chapter to apply certain ethical principles to persuasion, mainly those principles relating to truth telling and significant choice. To do so we will divide the ethical problems of persuasion into two broad categories: those relating to the course of action urged by the speaker and those relating to the means of persuasion employed. Both the course of action urged and the means of persuasion employed to gain its acceptance have effects on the persons addressed, and to a greater or lesser degree on the community beyond. It is these effects that give rise to the moral problems.

The course of action and the speaker's moral obligations

When a speaker urges his listeners to adopt a specific course of action, part of our ethical judgment of the speaker will be based on

[1] Yves Simon, **Philosophy of Democratic Government** (Chicago: University of Chicago Press, 1951), p. 109.

the possible consequences of the action proposed. The judgment is complicated by the fact that the consequences may be many and varied. For example, suppose a speaker tries to persuade his listeners to vote for a piece of legislation which will set up a local board of censors whose duty it will be to decide which movies will be shown in the community, which books will be placed on the library shelves or sold in the bookshops, and which magazines will be displayed at the counters. The effects of such legislation might be wide ranging. The actions of the board would probably affect the teaching in the schools; they certainly would affect the right of the people to choose their own information and entertainment, and hence they would affect the cultural level of the community, and its reputation in the larger society. Further, establishment of the board might encourage additional restrictive legislation or restrictive action on the part of public agencies, or it might precipitate violent response on the part of minority groups against such regulation. Certain effects would be short-term and other effects long-term. Some people would be affected directly, others indirectly; some seriously and others only slightly; and a few perhaps not at all.

Most actions of any significance have varied effects. While we most certainly must hold the persuader morally responsible for such effects as he intends to produce, it seems reasonable also to charge him with some responsibility for other effects which probably would also occur. We cannot, of course, hold the speaker responsible for all of the possible consequences of the policy he advocates. We cannot know what all the consequences might be, and even if we could know, we would not be able to judge with certainty whether or not our values would be served. But insofar as we can know or anticipate, the responsibility exists. For instance, to use analogy, when I am driving my car I am directly responsible for any damage, any ill effects, that result from my driving illegally, such as making an illegal turn. But even though I am driving "well within the law," I will also be held at least partially responsible for "accidents" which I could have avoided had I taken some precautions, had I anticipated that which could well have been anticipated, such as a slippery roadway, or children dashing into the street from an adjacent playground, though neither the slipperiness nor the children in the street would have been "my doing." A similar general principle should apply to speech. When a speaker persuades others to follow a course of action, such as voting to establish a censorship board, he is morally obligated to anticipate the consequences insofar as he is able, for he shares a moral responsibility for them—the long-term as well as the short-term, the indirect as well as the direct, consequences.

Not only must the persuader consider the possible effects of the proposal he advocates, but he must consider whether his proposal is the best that can be devised under the circumstances. To use the censorship board as an example of a course of action to be proposed, perhaps if the speaker included certain criteria for the selection of the board, the values of a free society would be better served. Or if the bill included safeguards against overzealous prosecutors, a greater good might be accomplished. Or perhaps the very proposal itself should be reexamined, and instead of urging the establishment of a censorship board, the speaker should advocate the enactment of safeguards against such a board being created at all!

It is not intended to suggest by this that there is one right or best policy for any given situation and that that policy can be known. What is meant is that an individual who urges a course of action should seriously consider alternative proposals as he searches for the best available plan, and that also he should so carefully think through his ethical responsibilities that he will even question his own basic premises and their relationship to the basic values he endorses.

Since social problems are so complex, and no one can foresee all the possible consequences of any particular proposal, there may be several different policies or programs that would be "good." While each proposal needs to be thoroughly analyzed, tested by public debate if possible, the best way to find a sound policy is to have several proposed and to have all thoroughly analyzed and compared so that an intelligent choice can be made among them. Though it is possible to make an ethical judgment on a single proposal after critical examination of it and the grounds for its acceptance, ethical judgments will usually be better where there are additional critically evaluated proposals to choose from.

We are touching here again, of course, on the marketplace of ideas principle. In a democratic society it is assumed that the best test (or at least the most workable test) of a social or political truth is its acceptance after public discussion, rather than the degree to which it conforms to certain criteria of truth or morality. The test has worked well. There are, however, dangers in relying too exclusively on public acceptance as the criterion of value. Rarely do we find a marketplace of ideas that provides the conditions for the kind of intellectual testing of propositions that adequately winnows the better from the worse. Rarely do we find a series of different proposals dealing with a particular problem, all presented at such a time and place that an audience can make the kind of comparison and judgment implied by the marketplace concept. Usually proposals are made one at a time, where the speaker is urging his own plan without having it exposed to comparison. In fact, too often such comparison is deliberately avoided. Although such piecemeal advocacy is vastly better than no advocacy at all, it does not provide audiences with an adequate perspective on the proposals made. Moreover, as was pointed out in the preceding chapter, there is a strong tendency for advocates to use the notion of the marketplace of ideas as a rationalization for their own partial, biased, and self-serving exhortations. They hold that as long as there is freedom of expression the various existing interests will plead their own causes; the result will be a number of different programs from which the people can choose. This supposedly absolves the individual advocate of responsibility for the consequences of his particular proposal, because his listeners, the public, have ample opportunity to choose another course of action.

It is ethically good that speakers provide alternative proposals among which listeners can choose. Insofar, however, as the individual advocate uses the existence of public discussion as a way of escaping responsibility for the possible consequences of what he himself is advocating, he is acting unethically. Furthermore, the lack of a sense of personal responsibility for what one proposes leaves the door open for endless misuse of the means of persuasion.

The ethical and the legal. A distinction should be drawn between what is legal for a speaker to do and what is ethical, although the two areas overlap. If a speaker urges his listeners to act in violation of duly established law we would, in most cases, judge the speaker to be acting unethically. The rule of law is essential to the well-being of men. As we have previously indicated, however, some laws may so violate our ethical standards that it becomes morally right to disobey them. The most soul-searching thought must nevertheless be given to the possible consequences of urging actions in opposition to established law, lest a worse rather than a better result be the consequence.

Our laws are designed to permit absolute freedom of thought and the maximum freedom of speech and action consistent with the same freedom for others. The laws are based on the assumption that such freedom provides the conditions under which men can most fully develop their potentialities. Freedom of expression, analysis of ideas in public discussion, confrontation in debate, and compromise among interests will result in the kind of society in which optimum development can take place. There is implied in this view a generous tolerance of different points of view, as well as the right to defend, and proselytize for, opinions which may be abhorrent to some members of society. Such freedom and tolerance, however, do not imply that men should not verbally oppose views they believe unsound or wrong. We have nothing less than a duty to point out misinformation, misleading statements, and unsound reasoning, and to try to anticipate the adverse consequences of proposals made. Without such criticism, freedom of speech does little to aid in the search for political and social truth.

The means of persuasion and the speaker's moral obligations

The method of persuasion used by a speaker can have effects fully as significant as the specific belief or action he advocates. The effects may be more subtle and less easy to describe, but they are of vital importance.

The adverse effects of language are recognized in our laws against false statements, defamation, and obscenity. Such use of language would certainly be termed unethical, not merely because it is illegal, but because such speech is damaging to individual human personalities and militates against harmonious and constructive relationships.

Legal restrictions of speech are kept at a minimum so that society can enjoy the benefits of the maximum freedom of expression. Recent trends in court decisions have been to reduce further such restrictions. Obscenity has simply become too difficult to define, and attitudes toward it have changed. Where defamation is concerned, in view of the need to preserve the right to criticize public officials, increasingly the plaintiff (especially if he is a public official) must prove malicious intent on the part of the critic. Intent, of course, is very difficult to establish. The reduction of restrictions, however, calls all the more for intelligent use of the freedom and thoughtful consideration of the moral responsibilities such freedom entails. The ethical issues of speech go far beyond the legal issues.

Persuasion and coercion. We have judged as morally acceptable the process of persuasion, where it is the awakening of a voluntary inclination to act. Coercion, on the other hand, since it conflicts with free choice, violates our criteria of the morally acceptable. Where the distinction between persuasion and coercion is clear-cut, we have little difficulty in making a moral judgment. One of the important ethical problems associated with persuasion, however, stems from the difficulty of deciding where persuasion ends and coercion begins. It is hard to determine whether there are forces operating from the outside or inside that are in a real sense "forcing" a particular choice. If, for example, a man fears reprisal for following a course of action, he may still be "free" to act or not, but it is a moot question whether his decision is the result of free choice or of coercion.

A similar question arises when the individual being persuaded is unaware of the "persuasive" forces operating in and on him. Most people probably are not conscious of the degree to which they respond because of established habits, prejudices, hopes, frustrations, or fears. When a persuader plays so subtly on prejudice, hopes, or fears that the listener is not conscious of the speaker's strategy, the listener's response can hardly be called the result of voluntary inclination. It must be kept in mind, to be sure, that urging people to adopt a course of action because certain of their hopes will be realized or their fears allayed, when done openly, certainly falls within the scope of legitimate persuasion. The key question is whether the listener is aware of what is happening to him, whether he is conscious, as far as possible, of the forces operating in and on him, and of the bases for his decision.

The very intensity of the process of persuasion can also bring it to the point of coercion. As Simon states, ". . . we have come to understand that propaganda, when carried beyond a certain point of intensity, becomes a process of psychical coercion"; and he adds, "Between moderate propaganda, which is a process of persuasion, and intensive propaganda, which is a process of psychical coercion, nobody can trace a clear line. The result is that psychical coercion, exercised by way of intensive propaganda, generally does not admit of legal identification." Intensive propaganda, Simon feels, is not consistent with democracy. "Of all conceivable forms of coercion, the only one which certainly conflicts with the essence of democracy is precisely the one which has the greatest resemblance to the democratic process of persuasion."[2]

Certain other uses of language, if they are not directly coercive, approach the coercive in that they lead away from a thoughtful and critical approach to decisions and may goad to shortsighted action and sometimes to angered retaliation. The profanity and obscenity, the vituperative language that became the trademark of the extreme campus radical of the past decade is illustrative. Certainly it was language degrading to the personalities addressed (and even more so the persons using it), contemptuous of existing values, and largely self-serving.

It is sometimes argued that profane and obscene—shocking—language serves a constructive purpose in that with its shock value it wrenches the rigid mind out of its complacent commitment to the familiar, shatters the habitual patterns of thought and action that form the resistant, brittle veneer of the culture, and thus provokes a reexamination of existing values. This may indeed occur at times, though it is doubtful that the most radical purveyors of shock language had such a sophisticated view of what they were doing, at least not until cultural critics began to analyze the protest phenomenon. Much protest has its basis in legitimate grievances, but as is the human wont, individual anger, frustration, and psychological need too often shape the vanguard of the movements into egotists to whom the protest, the shock, and the public drama become ends in themselves. But this should not divert our attention from the basic grievances which underlie movements for reform, and the necessity for change.

This much must be said about shock language. If it is to be used, it must be used with thoughtful consideration of its consequences, so that a perverted delight in the immediate attention and outrage does not obscure the alienation, the subversion of critical appraisal, the erosion of constructive use of language that can be fostered by indiscriminate use of the offensive terms. Surely it can rarely—let us be more definite—it can never be justified by the ego trip it provides the user; motives must be carefully evaluated.

[2] **Ibid.**, p. 127.

We must recognize that social institutions tend to develop a vested interest in things as they are, and that the leaders of such institutions are too often reluctant to make changes. There is usually a sense of security in the status quo. Sometimes unusual speech and action are needed to dramatize the depth and significance of the feelings of those who believe themselves to be inadequately served, indeed outright cheated, by the institutions in which they function: students by schools, workers by industry, ethnic minorities by the entrenched majority, the disadvantaged by governmental bureaucracies, and so on through the structure of society. But to make the unusually dramatic a principle of communication is to negate it; and to make the destructive a principle of action is to destroy the foundations upon which constructive social change takes place.

Where there is a considered judgment and a deep moral conviction that specific social change requires an element of coercion if it is to be achieved (and there are exceptional times when this may be the case), there are certain questions that must be asked, and answered in the affirmative, if the ethical principles espoused in this volume are to be met: (1) Have all the alternative means been explored, and within all reasonable limits tried, that would foster change by persuasion? (2) Is the change of sufficient moment to risk the damage that may be done to the democratic structure that we wish to preserve and enhance? To put it in more personal terms, will the hierarchy of values we will be setting up be supportive in the long run of the informed, self-determining individual? Will the dignity of the human personality be served? (3) Having achieved our specific goal, will we restore the democratic processes that foster self-determination through significant choice?

Only after the deepest self-searching and only with commitment to the larger good and with a keen sense of reluctance can we permit ourselves to violate duly established law. And further, we must be prepared to take the consequences of our action. There is no room here for calculated martyrdom or cheap publicity; there is only room for moral commitment against an established condition or code that we firmly believe violates human personalities.

The constituents of persuasion. Aristotle defined rhetoric as the art of discovering, in any particular case, the available means of persuasion. In delineating the means he stated: "Of the means of persuasion supplied by the speech itself there are three kinds. The first reside in the character (ethos) of the speaker; the second consist in producing a certain (the right) attitude in the hearer; the third appertain to the argument proper, insofar as it actually or seemingly demonstrates."[3] In other words, there is first the persuasive impact of the character and personality of the speaker, and second, the persuasive effect of appeals to the interests, needs, loves, hates, etc., of the audience. Third, there is the argument proper, in which evidence and reasoning from the evidence provide a rational basis for a conclusion. In subsequent rhetorical literature, the first two have generally been included under the heading of emotional appeal, and the third has been thought of as logical or rational appeal.

Textbooks for courses in public speaking and argumentation have traditionally separated the two types of appeals, referring to the former as persuasion and to the latter as argumentation. The term **argumentation** has been used to cover both processes, as may be seen in definitions taken from two early, widely used textbooks. Baker defines argumentation as ". . . the art of producing in the mind of someone else a belief in the ideas the speaker or writer wishes the hearer or reader to accept."[4] He thus included both kinds of appeals. Foster defined argumentation as "The communication of reasoning to other people for the purpose of convincing them and urging them to action. . . ."[5] He went on to say, however, that argumentation is concerned not only with reasoning, but with all other grounds for belief. It is safe to say that both these authors thought of the appeal to emotion as something to be added to the more basic and important rational appeal.

There is a tendency now to use **persuasion** as the more inclusive term. "Persuasion," say McBurney and Mills, "is a broader term than argumentation."[6] Minnick speaks of persuasion as "discourse . . . designed to win belief or stimulate action by employing all the factors that determine human behavior."[7] A distinction between argumentation and persuasion persists, however, emphasizing the differing ways in which people make up their minds, and the differing bases

[3] **The Rhetoric of Aristotle,** trans. Lane Cooper (New York: Appleton-Century, 1932), p. 8.
[4] George P. Baker, **Principles of Argumentation** (Boston: Ginn, 1895), p. 1.
[5] William T. Foster, **Argumentation and Debating,** rev. ed. (Boston: Houghton Mifflin, 1917), p. 123. The words quoted are italicized in the original.
[6] James H. McBurney and Glen E. Mills, **Argumentation and Debate,** 2nd ed. (New York: Macmillan, 1964), p. 166.
[7] Wayne C. Minnick, **The Art of Persuasion** (Boston: Houghton Mifflin, 1957), p. 33.

for belief and action. "Argumentation," says Freeley, "gives priority to logical appeals while taking cognizance of ethical and emotional appeals. Persuasion gives priority to ethical and emotional appeals while taking cognizance of logical appeals."[8] And McBurney and Mills: "In argumentation we study propositions, analysis, evidence, reasoning, attack and defense, etc. In persuasion we may study some of the same topics, but in addition we are likely to be concerned with the ethos of the source, motive appeals, the suggestive impact of style and delivery, and other nonlogical factors in the communicative process."[9] Windes and Hastings state: "In the task of influencing others, the advocate may employ a variety of approaches, but essentially he has access to two broad types: the **logical, or rational,** and the **psychological.** He may use each approach separately or both together."[10]

The above statements about argumentation and persuasion are presented to indicate the recognition of two general approaches to the influencing of attitudes and actions, approaches corresponding to the two general modes of response, the cognitive and the affective. If the approaches were sharply divided for purposes of definition and discussion, we should have (1) the approach which deals with objective evidence and processes of reasoning which are subject to publicly agreed-upon criteria of validity, and which form a rationally valid basis for accepting a proposition; and (2) the approach which deals with interests, needs, attitudes, and beliefs, which vary from person to person and to which the proposition must be related or adapted if it is to be accepted. Cognitive and affective responses are never isolated but always intermixed, one affecting the other (though one may predominate), and therefore persuasive appeals can never be wholly to the cognitive or wholly to the affective aspects of man's nature. Further, materials used in persuasion cannot be clearly divided on the basis of their appeals to the rational or the emotional in man. The same materials—say, for example, data on automobile accidents— may evoke an almost wholly emotional, unreflective response from one listener, while another listener will view the data as a basis for a rational inference about some aspect of automobile safety.

[8] Austin J. Freeley, **Argumentation and Debate** (San Francisco: Wadsworth, 1961), p. 7.
[9] McBurney and Mills, **Argumentation and Debate,** p. 166.
[10] Russel R. Windes and Arthur Hastings, **Argumentation and Advocacy** (New York: Random House, 1965), p. 24.

It is important to consider both the rational and the emotional side of behavior, since where decisions are difficult, requiring careful evaluation of data and reasoning from the data, undue emotional arousement and involvement may inhibit or distort the kind of objective appraisal needed for a decision that best serves the public good. It is the possibility of such emotional involvement at the expense of critical appraisal that forms the basis of much that is unethical in persuasion.

It is evident that if people are to exercise their capacities for informed, rational judgments, they must have the kind of information that makes this possible, and they must know the basic principles of valid inference. It is also evident that peoples' feelings, needs, attitudes, and beliefs enter into any judgment they make, and thus they should have an awareness of the role such factors play. Voluntary choice implies opportunity for informed critical judgment, with the emotional components considered and held, as far as possible, in proper perspective.

Since the cognitive and the affective in man are so intermingled, since even data cannot be systematically divided into that which evokes rational response and that which evokes emotional response, the rational and the emotional do not provide satisfactory categories for classifying material related to the means of persuasion. In the following discussion we will use a different classification, dividing the analysis of the means of persuasion into (1) a consideration of information used, and (2) a consideration of reasoning or inference making based on the information. Rational and emotional factors enter into both the informational and the inference-making aspects of persuasion.

The ethics of information

Communication content. Given the concept of the good presented here, persuasion is morally wrong when it misinforms, except in very unusual circumstances. Misinformation can be of various kinds. It is certainly not necessary for a speaker to make demonstrably false-to-fact statements in order to mislead his listeners. The information may, for instance, be incomplete; the selection of information may be biased; statistical units may be inadequately defined or incomplete; vague or ambiguous terminology, in which listeners find erroneous meanings, may be used; relationships may be implied between the issue under discussion and other issues when, in fact, no relevant relationship exists (e.g., in guilt by association); the issue may be given a false sense of urgency or a false sense of importance; highly emotionalized language may be used, which may distort meanings.

No speaker can say everything about any issue. All speaking must necessarily be incomplete. The ethical issues are whether the information presented is the most relevant available and is as complete as the particular circumstances make feasible. Further, since selection of material is inevitable, it must be made clear to the listeners what principles of selection are operating, what biases or special interests characterize the speaker, and what purposes are being served by the information given. Definitions must be adequate; statistical units must be defined and the assumptions underlying their use made explicit. The listeners must not be led to believe that they are getting a more complete and accurate picture than they really are. In addition, the subject must be placed in the proper perspective as far as its individual and social importance is concerned. In brief, the speaker must provide for the listener as adequate a grasp of the truth of the situation as is reasonably possible under the circumstances.

A question possibly occurs to the reader. After all, when one is persuading an audience to accept a point of view, one's purpose is to get that view accepted. Since it is impossible to say everything that is relevant, selection must take place and some bias is inevitable. Why, then, should one not slant the presentation to serve one's purpose? There is no easy answer to this question. Two completely sincere and honest people, holding different views on a particular issue, discussing it as objectively as possible, with no intent to slant or deceive, will nonetheless make quite different presentations.

The answer to the question hinges on our conception of the human personality and how it should determine its course of action. If we believe men should make informed, thoughtful, independent, critical choices, then if we are intellectually honest we will contribute to that kind of choice. Whatever slanting takes place will grow out of the nature of the material, evaluated, selected, organized, and delivered with the sincere intention of providing the most adequate basis for making choices. The material and the presentation will also reflect, and legitimately so, our concerns and feelings, our hopes and commitments.

The point can perhaps best be made by asking ourselves what kind of persuasive speeches we want to hear when we need to make a decision on an important issue. Granted that a significant part of any decision we make will be the pattern of attitudes we bring to the decision-making situation, we nevertheless want the kind of information that gives us a basis for genuine choice. We want to know the bias of the speaker, the meanings he attaches to terms, the assumptions that underlie his approach, the long-term values he is serving, and what he is leaving unsaid.

There are times, to be sure, when we may want to hear someone make the strongest case he can, selecting only such information as serves his purpose, but this is when we have the opportunity of hearing someone else make as thoroughly one-sided a case for the other side. There are times when we can welcome such bias, because in the situation it gives us additional insight into the attitudes of people holding differing views and the intensity of their commitment. As one writer has pointed out, if a minority dislike a program very intensely and a majority want it only moderately, a decision in favor of the majority may not be just.[11]

It is not assumed here that all audiences can be given all the information necessary for adequate decisions on all the kinds of problems facing a society. Where national problems are concerned, the voice of the people can express for the most part only approval or disapproval of broad policy, confidence or the lack of it in the leadership being provided. But there should be no less information provided, no less rigor of reasoning communicated, and no less democratic spirit fostered than circumstances make feasible. In speaking of the remoteness of national issues from the mind of the individual, and the importance of public understanding, Charles Frankel states:

> This [the remoteness of issues] does not mean that education and public spirit have no bearing on the success of democracy. It makes them more important, not less. If men are to make intelligent judgments about their leaders, they need a general understanding of the main drift of the issues, they need to have some shrewdness about the people they listen to, and they need to be able to tell the difference between sense and nonsense.[12]

[11] Robert Dahl, **A Preface to Democratic Theory** (Chicago: University of Chicago Press, 1956), p. 90.
[12] Charles Frankel, **The Democratic Prospect** (New York: Harper & Row [Colophon Books], 1962), p. 44.

People do not, however, develop the ability to distinguish sense from nonsense in the discussion of public affairs unless a good deal of sense is being talked. Partisan pleading and high-pressure salesmanship—of ideas as well as merchandise—are not conducive to an objective presentation of significant information and discussion of possible consequences and their relation to fundamental goals of our society. Thus, we have come to value highly the processes of public debate wherein there is confrontation of case with case, where advocates challenge each other's information and conclusions. Such confrontation produces the kind of information and criticism of conclusions that makes possible more intelligent choices on the part of the listeners.

As we have suggested, optimum confrontation is very seldom possible. As a consequence, the individual persuader has a moral obligation to present information needed for informed, independent choice. Whether he does this will depend on the value he assigns to his listeners' opportunity for such choice, not simply in the sense of how wisely or independently he thinks the listeners might be able to choose in a given instance, but how significant he feels it to be that human personalities not only retain but further develop the desire and capacity for critical, self-determining decision.

The listeners' responsibility. Thus far we may have appeared to place all the ethical responsibility on the speaker, absolving the listener of obligations to be skeptical, to inform himself, or to evaluate critically the speaker who may be attempting to manipulate him. Can a speaker not legitimately assume that his hearers can and should inform themselves on issues of significance to them, that they should seek out discussions of various points of view so as to be able to compare and evaluate? Can he not assume that his listeners should anticipate consequences and relate them to the values they want to see realized?

The problem is a relative one, of course. The speaker's responsibility in any given instance will depend upon circumstances. If his presentation is a part of a symposium where other points of view based on other information are being presented, then certainly the speaker can to a large extent depend upon the other speakers to furnish the complementary information which will provide the bases for intelligent decision making. Much also depends on the educational level of the audience, the availability of the information needed, and the ability of the audience to make use of the available sources of information. The more the speaker is the sole source of information, the sole persuader, the greater his personal responsibility to his listeners for providing the bases for sound and independent thought. His obligation will be proportionate to what his listeners need in order to make informed, independent judgments.

Our emphasis here is on the ethical responsibilities of the speaker. The nature of the audience does not relieve the speaker of ethical obligations, although it may modify them. The members of the audience, as responsible citizens of a democratic society, have an ethical obligation to be informed and critical. If more audiences would fulfill this moral obligation, the result would be higher ethical standards in public communication. There is a temptation for the speaker to be lax when his audience lacks critical standards.

It must be emphasized, however, that failure on the part of the listeners to inform themselves and to evaluate the speaker critically in no way absolves the speaker of his responsibilities. If anything, it increases them.

Word meanings. Directly related to the problem of information is that of the meaning of words. To what extent is the persuader responsible for the meanings that his listeners attach to his words? He wants them to find certain meanings; if they misunderstand, who is to blame? One should not place all the responsibility on the speaker, but if he respects the integrity of his hearers, if he respects their right to think for themselves, he will accept the obligation to select his words so that there is the maximum probability of correct interpretation.

This is not to say that vagueness and ambiguity are wrong in themselves. To a certain extent they cannot be avoided. There are also instances of their legitimate use. If a speaker seeks to stimulate his listeners to feelings of national pride (certainly an acceptable purpose if done with prudence), he must realize that for different people different aspects of their national life are cause for pride, and the speaker can rightfully permit each listener to identify with that which is most meaningful to him. Where rigorous thought is needed, however, where decisions are being made on specific issues, such personal interpretations may be highly misleading, and the speaker has an ethical obligation to minimize them. If ambiguity is unavoidable, it should be made explicit. Where vagueness is unavoidable, the speaker should not claim more specificity than the terms warrant.

Moreover, the speaker must consider his emotional impact on a particular audience. He cannot escape responsibility by pleading that his words are not intended to arouse emotion or that other audiences do not so respond to them. The speaker is obligated to anticipate to the best of his ability the possible effect of his words on his listeners. It is not, as has been amply emphasized, that emotion is to be avoided, but that the emotions to be aroused are those which will motivate to objective appraisal of information and purposes, and which will foster independent and constructive action.

Value assumptions. It is not always apparent from the persuader's expressed purpose, or his means of persuasion, just what long-term goals he seeks or what fundamental values he serves. This is part of the vital information needed by the listeners if they are to make intelligent decisions. A speaker, therefore, is not meeting his ethical obligations unless he reveals his own value assumptions, the long-term as well as the short-term objectives he is furthering.

The ethics of reasoning

The purpose of persuasion is to change attitudes and beliefs and subsequent overt behavior. The process of changing beliefs involves some movement or progression of thought—some element of inference or reasoning, that is, proceeding from premises (however incompletely stated) to a conclusion. There are widely varying degrees of rigor in making inferences. Even when the persuasion is effected by the direct emotional impact of words or visual images that evoke favorable or unfavorable responses, there is at least some progression of thought, some truncated process of drawing a conclusion on the part of the listener.

However much or little logical reasoning may enter into the making of inferences, all of us like to think of ourselves as reasoning human beings. Our tendency to rationalize, to come up with "reasons" for doing something we already want to do, is one obvious indication of our desire to be guided by thoughtful consideration of alternative actions and their consequences. When we decide to see a movie instead of studying, we probably convince ourselves that we need the relaxation, that we will be able to study better if we take a break, that the movie has "educational" value, or that one should not neglect one's social life entirely. All of these reasons may have genuine merit. What makes the reasoning rationalization is that we had a strong inclination, or had really decided, to go to the movie first; the reasons came after the fact, and made us feel better.

The desire people have to feel that they are rational provides opportunities for the persuader. By making his persuasive appeals **appear** to be logical, and by helping his listeners rationalize a point of view that their self-interest prompts them to take, he can more successfully influence behavior. The use of "reasoning" in persuasion, then, raises ethical problems.

Levels of inference. It is helpful to think of persuasive appeals as falling into three broad categories, based on the process of inference involved. These categories overlap; the inferences rarely occur in pure and isolated form, but they are distinct enough to provide general classifications. First, there are the directly associational appeals, where probably no conscious inference is made. This is illustrated in advertising by the pretty girl sipping a drink or the rugged male smoking his favorite filter-tip cigarette. Nothing is said about what conclusion should be drawn, but some effect is presumed. In speeches this category is illustrated by emotion-laden words or descriptions that arouse strong feelings which then become transferred to another idea or person.

The second category includes the use of reasons for believing or doing, but the reasons do not provide rational grounds for drawing the conclusion presented. For example: "You should use NoSmel because it will make you socially successful"; "You should vote for Richard Roe because he believes in the principles of Americanism."

The last group includes the use of reasons which do provide rational grounds for the conclusion drawn. "You should buy Aircraft Incorporated stock because it has steadily appreciated in value since the formation of the corporation, and present buying trends indicate continued demand for its products." The purchase of the stock may not be a profitable step, but the conclusion is rationally warranted.

The types of appeal are not usually so clearly recognizable or classifiable. In actual discourse the conclusion may be removed some distance from the premises, vague and emotion-arousing terms may appear in the premises, and spurious and sound reasoning may be intertwined.

Ethical issues. There are two major questions in the use of reasoning in persuasive speeches. One is whether the persuader attempts to lead his listeners to believe that he is employing greater rigor of reasoning than actually is the case, and the other, which is closely related, is whether the persuader is using the evidence that is available and is reasoning as rigorously as the materials permit and the sophistication of his audience warrants.

There is generally no pretense that direct association is reasoning at all, so that ethical judgment of its use does not turn on its soundness or rigor. The ethical question with respect to the direct impact of words and visual images turns rather on the place of such persuasion in the larger context of the persuasive speech. It is most certainly not unethical to arouse pleasant associations in connection with the proposal one wishes to see adopted. If, however, the pleasant associations are misleading, or if they are used to the exclusion of more rational bases for judgment, or if their use fosters decision making mainly on the basis of pleasant or unpleasant associations, then such persuasion becomes unethical. The criterion of ethical speech, as we have said, is whether it fosters in men informed, critical choice. Any means of persuasion that stands in the way of, or that leads away from, or militates against such a process of arriving at choices is to that degree unethical, except in the most unusual circumstances.

The use of spurious reasoning with the implicit or explicit implication that rationally justifiable grounds are being given for the choice urged is plainly and unequivocally wrong. This is plain deception, and it fosters unsound decision making. Too, it reveals disrespect for the listeners.

It is not always easy, of course, to establish whether reasoning is sound. Where the process of drawing conclusions is so clear-cut and the terms used so unambiguous that the established principles of reasoning can clearly be applied, judgment of the soundness of the argument is relatively simple.

There are many instances of reasoning, however, where the principles of sound induction and deduction are not so readily applicable. Suppose the persuader is reasoning inductively—that is, drawing a conclusion about a class of people or events on the basis of verifiable knowledge of a sample of the class. How large must his sample be, how qualified his generalization or conclusion, in order that it can be considered justified? No simple, generally applicable answer is possible. The warrantability of the conclusion in a given case would depend on several factors, such as the amount of data available, the kind of data (sometimes one sample is enough, sometimes a large number is needed), and the importance of the issue to which the conclusion is relevant. If the conclusion could have serious consequences for those affected, only the most rigorous reasoning would be ethically acceptable. The same principle would apply if the persuader were reasoning deductively—that is, drawing a conclusion from two or more premises. The premises used in persuasive discourse are for the most part only probable, and the terms used are as a rule not totally unambiguous. For example, if high taxes generally bring about a slump in business, and taxes are now very high, can one reasonably conclude that we are soon to experience a business slump? Judgment about the adequacy of such reasoning must take into consideration the probable truth of the premises, the probable meaning of the terms for the audience, and the significance of the conclusion to the people affected by it.

The fundamental ethical issue is whether the reasoning employed by the speaker is such that it contributes to making the most constructive decisions, given the information available, and whether in the long run such reasoning would contribute to the preservation of our basic values.

The question might arise whether the persuader is obligated to attempt to carry his listeners through a process of sound reasoning when they are not able to understand or appreciate it. A tightly reasoned argument that is lost on the listeners certainly has no particular ethical value. The fact that listeners do not recognize sound evidence and reasoning, however, is no warrant whatever for the use of spurious evidence and reasoning; but it may and should influence the way in which the evidence and reasoning are presented. They will need to be presented in a simplified manner that is meaningful to the listeners.

The persuader bears an ethical obligation to study the principles of reasoning and their application in discourse, so that he can test his own arguments for validity. We have said that the persuader is obligated to inform himself adequately on his subject, to anticipate possible consequences of his proposals, and to analyze, as far as he can, his own motivations. No less is he obligated to examine his own reasoning for its soundness, lest he mislead his listeners and foster the kind of thinking that is inconsistent with the personality we value.

Errors in reasoning. An error in reasoning is simply the drawing of a conclusion not warranted by the evidence or the propositions from which the conclusion is drawn. It is not unethical for a speaker to make such an error if he has conscientiously studied the processes of inference and has tried to reason as soundly as possible. If, however, a speaker pretends to be reasoning validly and is not, he is speaking unethically.

There are many types of faulty inference (commonly called fallacies) that lend themselves to use in persuasion. Used as arguments they have a certain surface plausibility, and the fault may be difficult to detect in the context of the other statements that surround them. Fallacies are discussed at length in most books on argumentation and debate, and in introductory texts on logic, and will be touched on only briefly here to indicate how they may function in persuasion. The student is urged to familiarize himself thoroughly with the sources of error in reasoning.

Perhaps the fallacies most commonly and deliberately used in persuasion are those that beg the question or ignore it. A common but oversimplified form of begging the question would be illustrated by someone arguing that the lack of discipline in schools is the result of the permissive attitudes of educators, since permissiveness on the part of teachers always results in poor discipline. The original assertion and the "proof" might be separated by a lengthy discourse.

The fallacies of ignoring the question (also called the fallacies of irrelevant evidence) are somewhat more bizarre. They are still often referred to by their Latin titles. They include:

Argumentum ad hominem—an appeal directed at the beliefs or character of an individual instead of at the subject matter in controversy; usually an attack on the person who advocates the proposition.

Argumentum ad populum—an appeal to the passions or prejudices of a people, thereby obscuring or avoiding the real issue.

Argumentum ad ignorantiam—a fallacious attempt to shift the burden of proof, such as stating, "This is true because you cannot prove it is not true."

Argumentum ad vericundiam—an appeal to the respect or admiration people have for an authority or great name.

Argumentum ad judicium—ignoring the real question and attempting to prove that most men believe so and so; that is, assuming that the general belief cannot be wrong.

Argumentum ad baculum—an appeal to force or the use of threats.

Other common fallacies include those where the conclusion covers new material and no attempt is made to show a cause-and-effect connection; where the assumption is made that because one event precedes another in time, one is the cause of the other; where the assumption is made that what is true of a part is true of the whole; where words are used whose meanings shift in the course of the argument.

Propagandistic devices. The term **propaganda,** much like the term **persuasion** itself, has various meanings. Interpreted broadly enough, any attempt to change attitudes or beliefs may be thought of as propagandistic. More commonly, however, the word **propaganda** is reserved for the persuasive methods that are primarily manipulative. The propagandist wants to influence the attitudes and beliefs of listeners or readers for his own ends. He does not seek to encourage informed, critical appraisal of his statements or purposes.

There has been much discussion of propaganda, its nature and use in our society, and there have been various characterizations of propaganda methods. The following summary description is simply illustrative, pointing up the essentially nonrational nature of propaganda. It is included here to suggest the relationship between propaganda and persuasion. "The propagandist," says Evjen, "in order to get people to act in a desired way will often employ such techniques as:

1. **Omission**—deliberately ignoring those facts that would damage the case.
2. **Derision**—using caricature and ridicule in order to get people to form opinions without examining the evidence.
3. **Transfer**—using a well-known symbol, like the cross or the flag, as authority in order to suggest that they sanction or endorse opinion.
4. **Falsification**—deliberately using untruths, and excessive exaggeration.
5. **Evasion**—using positive symbols like truth, freedom, democracy, Americanism, honor and Christian in order that by identifying one's cause with them opinions will be formed.

6. **Emotional appeal**—identifying opposing ideas with fears, hates and prejudices so as to create opposition without examining the facts.
7. **False reasoning**—using unwarranted assumptions, begging the question, the rule of the excluded middle, circularity and insufficient evidence.
8. **Association**—use of testimonials, plain folk language, and "the best people read it" approach in order to induce others to think and do likewise."[13]

It will be noted that these methods embody several of the fallacies just described. The common intent running through the methods is, obviously, the attempt to avoid presenting the kind of information that gives the listener a comprehensive picture of the issue under discussion, to avoid providing a basis for objective, critical thought about the issue, to avoid independent decision. The end is manipulation—triggering springs of action in the listener so that he acts without thoughtful consideration of various alternatives and their consequences.

As described above, and used as manipulative devices, these methods are morally wrong by the ethical standards proposed in this volume for the simple reason that they violate the concept of the self-determining personality. This is not to say that all such propagandistic methods are always morally wrong; qualifications were set forth in the preceding chapter. But if we believe that the individual should have the maximum opportunity to exercise his right to and capacity for free choice—significant choice—then we are obligated to provide good reasons for the choices we advocate, reasons which will permit critical judgment among alternatives. Our freedom of action is essentially proportionate to our knowledge of alternatives and their possible consequences. That such freedom is always limited should only impel us to maximize it whenever possible.

In short, persuasion which fosters significant choice, which awakens voluntary inclination based on such choice, is consistent with the concept of the good on which our discussion of the ethics of communication is based. The human condition is mainly improved, it would seem, through the agency of the more farsighted men of good will who

---

[13] Henry O. Evjen, "An Analysis of Some of the Propaganda Features of the Campaign of 1940," **The Southwestern Social Science Quarterly,** XXVII (December 1946), 247.

persuade others to join them in constructive action. The means as well as the ends must serve the human personality.

Related readings

Brown, James A. C. **Techniques of Persuasion.** Baltimore: Penguin, 1963.

Fearnside, W. Ward, and William B. Halther. **Fallacy, The Counterfeit of Argument.** Englewood Cliffs, N.J.: Prentice-Hall, 1959.

Haiman, Franklyn S. "The Rhetoric of the Streets: Some Legal and Ethical Considerations," **Quarterly Journal of Speech,** LIII (April 1967), 99–114.

Johannesen, Richard. **Ethics and Persuasion.** New York: Random House, 1967.

Miller, Gerald R., and Thomas R. Nilsen. **Perspectives on Argumentation.** Chicago: Scott, Foresman, 1966. Pp. 176–197.

Nilsen, Thomas R. "Free Speech, Persuasion, and the Democratic Process," **Quarterly Journal of Speech,** XLIV (October 1958), 235–243.

FIVE

On the "optimific" word

Most of us make relatively few public speeches on significant issues, but all of us talk to someone almost every day of our lives. As we said in Chapter 1, our words affect other people in many ways as we pass the time of day, converse and discuss, instruct, direct, plead, and persuade. Moreover, what we fail to say is sometimes as important as what we do say. This chapter is mainly concerned with the ethics of informal speech communication, the interpersonal communications of daily life.

On whether we should always do the best we can

Ethical issues stand forth sharply when great problems are confronted, when reputations and lives are at stake. Ethical issues are less easy to discern in the routine speech and actions of every day, where the common misunderstandings, frustrations, conflicts, and injured feelings are experienced. How we approach the problem of the moral responsibilities of informal speech depends upon our concept of ethical obligation and how far such obligation extends. There is no disagreement among us, for instance, about whether we should help someone we come upon who is in trouble, and whom we can help.

There would be disagreement, however, about how far we should go in looking for people to help. Further, we might all agree that in a given case we should not go out of our way to say something unpleasant, but should we go out of our way to say something pleasant? The problem we have before us is not so much whether we should do the good rather than the bad, but whether when confronted with two alternatives both of which are good (or at least, neither of which is bad), we are under obligation to do the better. Do we always have the obligation to do, or say, that which maximizes the good?

This is a question to which philosophers have devoted a good deal of attention. A brief look at some contemporary views will make the problem clearer. Kurt Baier states:

> We do not have the duty to do good to others or to ourselves, or to others and/or to ourselves in a judicious mixture so that it produces the greatest possible amount of good in the world. We are morally required to do good only to those who are actually in need of our assistance. The view that we always ought to do the optimific act, or whenever we have no more stringent duty to perform, would have the absurd result that we are doing wrong whenever we are relaxing. . . .[1]

A similar point of view is taken by D. J. B. Hawkins, who distinguishes between acts that are morally obligatory and those that are not. He says, "Besides the sense of right in which it means 'obligatory,' there is a sense in which it means 'morally permissible,' and the sense in which it means 'morally desirable.' " He says further:

> Too many philosophers, including Kant, have written as if it were always obligatory to do the best possible act in the circumstances. But this is contrary to our moral consciousness and would impose an intolerable burden on human nature. In ordinary circumstances we recognize a certain standard below which we must not fall; the choice of the better is laudable but not strictly obligatory.[2]

Other philosophers suggest that indeed it is a man's obligation to do the best possible in the circumstances. Garnett recognizes three levels of obligation or three requirements of morally right conduct.

[1] Kurt Baier, **The Moral Point of View: A Rational Basis of Ethics** (Ithaca: Cornell University Press, 1958), p. 203.
[2] D. J. B. Hawkins, **Man and Morals** (New York: Sheed and Ward, 1960), p. 25.

He summarizes, putting the types of obligation in ascending order of importance:

> We may sum up the requirements for completest possible fulfillment of man's potentialities for voluntary control of conduct—the moral requirements—as they follow from our analysis, in the following three principles. (1) Act as required by personal prudence, except when this would be contrary to the requirements of personal and group loyalty and impartial good will. (2) Act as required by personal and group loyalty, except when this would be contrary to the requirements of impartial good will. (3) Act always as required by impartial good will.[3]

When Garnett speaks of personal and group loyalty, he is speaking of duties to "the group, and to individuals to whom one has special commitments. . . ." Impartial good will goes beyond such individuals and groups to man in general. Garnett explains:

> The highest stage of ethical conduct is only reached with the development of the capacity for impartial or disinterested good will, unsupported by the self-regarding elements in group loyalty. This comes with abstract thinking about the nature of man, as man, with seeing the common humanity in all men, with an imaginative entering into the feelings of other persons, even of those outside the circle of the groups to which one is bound by natural loyalties.[4]

Rader is yet more explicit about the obligatoriness of what Baier calls "the optimific act." In Rader's words:

> It seems to me self-evident that we ought to perform any act the total content and consequences of which stand higher in the scale of intrinsic value than those of any other act which might have been chosen. Instead of yielding to some bias in favor of a less valuable alternative, we should bring about the most good and the least evil in our power. There is no more fundamental principle of ethics than this. If we do not accept this principle, we can have no basis for an objective teleological ethics, whether for an individual or society.[5]

---

[3] A. Campbell Garnett, "Good Reasons in Ethics: A Revised Conception of Natural Law," **Mind,** LXIX (July 1960), 360.
[4] **Ibid.,** 359.
[5] Melvin Rader, **Ethics and Society** (New York: Holt, 1950), p. 212. In his later book, **Ethics and the Human Community** (New York: Holt, Rinehart and Winston, 1965), Rader is apparently not so explicit on this point, but the above statement does not appear to be inconsistent with the later work.

Smith and Debbins, taking a similar view, suggest that perhaps the notion of "better" or "worse" should be the ethical criterion. It implies that we should always be trying to do the better. "There is no top or bottom," say Smith and Debbins, "to the moral scale; there is only the indefinitely expansible middle." As they sum it up: "When you stop being better, you stop being good."[6]

Another man, not a philosopher but one whose idealism and dedication to public service earned him the respect of the world, stated simply, "In any human situation, it is cheating not to be, at every moment, one's best."[7]

The differences among the above views do not imply that the first two philosophers are any less interested in morally right behavior than those in the latter group, but reflect differences in interpretation of ethical responsibility. The first group wants to reserve the term "obligation" to apply to certain clear-cut and significant ethical demands or requirements, all the while recognizing the desirability or laudability of doing the better thing when alternatives present themselves. The latter group of philosophers does not attempt to draw quite the same distinctions, but assumes a general moral responsibility to do that which is better, which would include both the desirable and the obligatory.

There would probably be little difference in the behavior based on either point of view; to say that an act is laudable would surely be to exert moral pressure in its favor. To this writer it appears, however, that the latter point of view is more consistent and tenable. Doing the "optimific" thing would not place an undue burden on anyone if he approached his obligations with humility and a sense of proportion; it might be important for the individual to relax from time to time to conserve or build up his strength for the better overall performance of his duties. Moreover, just as goodness can helpfully be thought of in relative terms, so also can ethical obligation. In general, the greater the possible good of an act, the greater the obligation to perform or support it (balancing it, of course, against other demands); the greater the evil of an act, the greater the obligation to avoid or oppose it.

[6] T. V. Smith and William Debbins, **Constructive Ethics** (Englewood Cliffs, N.J.: Prentice-Hall [Spectrum Books], 1948), p. 116.
[7] Dag Hammarskjöld, **Markings** (New York: Knopf, 1965), p. 156.

On opportunities for saying the better thing

The question whether we should always do the optimific thing is
particularly relevant to a discussion of the ethics of speech. In no
other area of conduct do we so continuously have an effect on other
people, and so often have a choice of doing (for speech is an act)
what is more or less good. With almost every statement or nonverbal
cue, some shade of meaning can add to or detract from the well-
being of the communicants, increase or decrease the harmony of
their relationships, encourage or discourage further constructive interaction.

The problem of saying the better thing can perhaps be seen most
clearly in the situation where a speaker is urging an audience to adopt
a specific course of action. There might be many, many degrees of
value in what the speaker seeks to accomplish, from the very good to
the very bad. Also, there might be degrees of value in the means of
persuasion used, in the sense that the means of persuasion might
contribute to intelligent choice making on the part of the listeners
or to impulsive, thoughtless action. Everything we have said about
truth telling, significant choice, and persuasion would be applicable
in making ethical judgments about public addresses. In public speaking the optimific thing, according to our criteria, would be to speak
as truthfully as possible, provide as much opportunity as feasible for
informed, critical choices on the part of the listeners, arouse the most
appropriate feelings relative to the purposes sought, and in general
to speak so as to contribute the most to the intellectual and cultural
life of the audience—never forgetting, of course, humility and a sense
of proportion.

Our primary purpose in this chapter, however, as we have indicated,
is to consider the ethical aspects of informal, interpersonal communication rather than what is usually known as public speaking. For
purposes of discussion the areas of informal communication will be
divided into interpersonal and family relationships, conversation and
discussion, and work relationships.

Interpersonal and family relationships. Morally good communications are those which best preserve the integrity of the ego, contribute to personal growth, and harmonize relationships. These ends
are served by communications which, in addition to providing
the information needed in a given situation, permit and encourage

the expression of thought and feeling, and reveal respect for the person as a person.

The more the well-being of one individual is tied to the attitudes and actions of another, the more crucial the nature of the interpersonal communication becomes. The more closely people live and work together the more nonverbal factors enter into communication and the more individual attitudes and expectations influence the response. For example, replying to a stranger's query about the location of the nearest station, and replying to a friend's question about the quality of his work, involve vastly different degrees of emotional involvement. The dictionary meaning of the words will suffice for the stranger, and the verbal interchange will be fleeting and soon forgotten. The reply to the friend will get some of its meaning from what has been said in the past, from the degree of mutual confidence, the emotional and professional security of each, expectations of future relationships, the apparent attitude of the friend at the time of the question, and so on through many facets of the relationship. The problem would be to sense the feelings behind the question, to combine honesty with respect for the friend's sensitivities, to maintain mutual respect and confidence.

The opportunities for moral choice in interpersonal communication run through all our interactions with people, from our talking to the youngest of children to our talking to the oldest of adults, within and outside of our families, and in all the varied kinds of activities in which we engage. A child is affected by the talking directed both to him and to others around him. As Overstreet puts it: ". . . unless some unusual influence enters to change the pattern, most children grow up talking as the adults around them talk. If the speech they hear from their first moment of consciousness is undistinguished and banal, theirs is likely to become so. If the speech they hear is fretful with irritation and self-pity; or is an instrument of malice; or is loaded with dogmatism and prejudice, their own is likely to become so. Mediocrity is marvelously transmissible by contagion, and never more so than in the area of speech."[8]

Communications with children are particularly instructive because the need for receptivity on the part of the adult is seen so readily. The principle remains important in adult communications, although

[8] Harry Overstreet, **The Mature Mind** (New York: Norton, 1949), p. 55.

the needs are not so obvious and the responsibility is shared. When the adult and the child are communicating, the most important factor is the receptiveness of the adult to the thoughts and feelings of the child. The point can perhaps be made most dramatically by borrowing an example from the writing of Jurgen Ruesch.[9] In his book **Disturbed Communication,** Dr. Ruesch is concerned with communication and emotional problems and considers among other things communication situations that are frustrating. Frustration is often caused by a tangential reply. To borrow one of Ruesch's examples, and adapting it to our present purpose, suppose a mother is standing in her clean living room waiting for the bridge club when little Johnny comes in, a wiggling night crawler cupped in his muddy hands. "Look, Mommy, I caught a worm!" The mother's agitation would be understandable, and if she were to reply, "Get that worm out of here and go wash your dirty hands," we would not be surprised. But if she were to do so, what would be the effect on the boy? He is full of enthusiasm and wants to share an exciting experience, but he perceives in the response no recognition or appreciation of what he is trying to say; the mother as the receiver of the communication "disregards the intent of the sender," as Ruesch puts it. The child's communication is unconsummated; his feelings are ignored and he is unsatisfied, frustrated. No great harm, perhaps, but if he experiences many similar failures of communication, he will probably cease to attempt to share his enthusiasms and say only what he is sure will get a favorable response. Very probably, the difficulty many of us have as adults in sharing our feelings is a result of such unconsummated communication experiences, the early frustrations of attempting to communicate. Communication to us may not be satisfying and rewarding.

Suppose the mother in the story above were to hold back her almost automatic "Get that thing out of here," and even if for a moment, share the child's enthusiasm, reflect his joy, before sending him out. Suppose she were to say, "Oh, isn't that a wonderful worm? Where did you find him?" and after a reply were to say, "I think the worm will be much happier back in the flower garden, so put him there as soon as you can, and then wash your hands." The child may not particularly like this course of action either, but at least he has succeeded in communicating his feelings; someone has responded to his intent. If

[9] Jurgen Ruesch, **Disturbed Communication** (New York: Norton, 1957), pp. 54–55.

such responses to his feelings are frequent, he will find communication a satisfying experience; he will find fulfillment through communication.

It is good that healthy personality growth should be encouraged. If parents are aware of what they are doing, it is surely morally wrong for them to frustrate the communication experiences of their children, just as it would be wrong for them to frustrate other experiences essential to the most adequate development of the personality. This is not to say that every individual instance of unsatisfying communication is a wrong against the child; it is impossible for any human being to be appropriately responsive all of the time. The cumulative effect of many experiences shapes the personality, but it is through attention to the individual instances that communication can be improved.

Later in the child's life the interactions are more complex, the communication situations more varied, and the opportunities for good or bad communications more numerous. Receptivity to communication and ego supportive response are still major needs. It often becomes more difficult, however, for the parent to respond appropriately as the child grows older because the parent's position or authority, or role, is more directly challenged, and the parent feels on the defensive. Not infrequently, the result is that the parent responds by turning the tables, so to speak, and putting the young person on the defensive. Suppose, for example, that a young man asks his father for the car, and the father replies, "You had it last night, didn't you?" The father may be hesitant to say "No" directly and explicitly, and avoids responsibility for a forthright reply by placing the boy in a position made blameworthy by implication, where he has to defend his request. There is no attempt to encourage an explanation of what is probably a request going beyond established rules; there is revealed no sensitivity to the need the young man may be experiencing, or the unusual circumstances that may have led to the asking. It is not the sort of reply that fosters confidence in the possibility of solving a problem through talk. Communication tends to be blocked. A response such as the following might provide a very different basis for communication and interaction. "In view of our understanding about the car, I know you wouldn't ask for it unless something special had come up. Would you tell me about it so we can talk it over?" The father may not give him the use of the car; that is not the immediate point. The second kind of response explicitly recognizes that special needs may arise;

it recognizes the individuality and integrity of the boy; it supports rather than threatens his ego—it is much less likely to put him on the defensive. To be sure, much depends upon the tone of voice and the general spirit in which the interchange takes place, the past relationships, and other relevant circumstances in the situation.

Communication among adults is affected by similar factors. Everyone brings to each communication situation his own perceptions and needs. In situations where he is emotionally involved he sees varying degrees of support or threat to his self-concept; and where there is threat there is defense.

Defensiveness is one of the most pervasive obstacles to effective communication, and it points to the heart of the ethical requirements of interpersonal communication. **Morally right speech is that which opens up channels for mind to reach mind, and heart to reach heart.** It is speech that shows respect for the person as a person, whatever his age, status, or relationship to the speaker; it reveals respect for his ideas, feelings, intentions, and integrity; it reveals receptiveness to his communications, and it encourages self-expression. Such speech creates conditions in which the personality can function most freely and fully.

Most of us, to a far greater extent than we realize, defend ourselves against real or imagined slights, and cause others to do the same. Through hasty rebuttals, evasive and indirect replies, we protect ourselves, subtly attack others, and build walls between ourselves and others, reducing the state of well-being and the harmony of relationships.

More than personal feelings, of course, must be considered in informal communications. Our ethics must do justice to every side of man's nature. Therefore, in informal as well as formal speech we must be concerned about truth telling and significant choice, about respect for intelligent thought, appropriate emotional tone, and proper use of language. In informal speech we probably reveal most clearly the intellectual and cultural standards we set for ourselves.

"To misuse the word is to show contempt for man." We have an ethical choice in the words we use whenever we talk to others; we can choose the better or the less good.

Conversation and discussion. In group situations where mutual or public problems are being discussed, much opportunity exists for contributing to the greater good by saying that which adds to the well-being of people concerned, and which fosters constructive discussion. There is opportunity to promote friendliness, respect for personality, objectivity toward ideas and people, interest in issues, and respect for evidence and for the rational weighing of alternatives.

We all know, of course, that we ourselves are friendly; it is other people who don't always know it! The added phrase that welcomes another's presence or seeks another's opinion can communicate feelings of friendliness and concern that might otherwise be lost. Careful listening to another's views, with a genuine attempt to understand before agreeing or disagreeing, reveals respect for the person and his thought. Objectivity, an unwillingness to pass hasty judgment, an openness toward new information or interpretations, a hospitality toward opposing ideas, all help to set a tone that fosters cooperative thought and constructive human relations. This much, of course, we know, but too often we lack the desire or the will to make the effort to do the best we can.

In an earlier chapter we stated that to be ethical we must be rational, which implies some understanding of ourselves and of others so that we can intelligently consider various influences that may be operating within ourselves and others in a particular communication situation. This permits us to adapt to or compensate for those influences, at least to a degree.

Further, if discussion is to be productive, it is essential that we understand and are able to utilize the procedures of organized, purposive group thinking. Sound methods must be employed, and attitudes conducive to effective participation must be fostered. The decision-making procedure commonly used in discussion, where there is a sequence of thought from the statement of a problem through definition of terms, suggestion of courses of action, and final selection, is illustrative of rational procedure. In this sense the rational becomes the ethical because it contributes to the more adequate fulfillment of human purposes.[10] So also with the attitudes of permissiveness, objectivity, and open-mindedness, which have strong ethical implications because of what they contribute to the furthering of the human

---

[10] Other writers have also spoken to this point: "The achievement of methodological abilities and attitudes corresponding to these principles of method is equivalent to the achievement of some of the fundamental traits of a democratically moral character." R. Bruce Raup, George E. Axtelle, Kenneth D. Benne, and B. Othanel Smith, **The Improvement of Practical Intelligence** (New York: Harper, 1950), p. 205.

interests involved. Proper attitudes are important both to the emotional well-being of the group and to the soundness of the thought processes and the ultimate decision.

There is also the opportunity to influence more directly the personal well-being of others and the effectiveness of the group through creating the conditions under which other people can more readily express what they feel and know. When we think of communicating, we ordinarily have in mind the problem of directing a communication to someone so that he will understand us. But of equal and sometimes greater importance is the process of receiving communications from others. This means more than passively listening; it means creating conditions that make it easy for others to communicate with us. It means making ourselves more receptive to communication, more "communicatable with." If we believe in the optimum fulfillment of human personalities, it follows that we must strive to create the psychological conditions which make it possible for those with whom we communicate to give more effective expression to their thoughts and feelings.

Almost everything said or done in conversation or discussion has some effect on the feelings or attitudes of the participants and on the quality of the thought emerging. In casual conversation the feelings are most important; no particular intellectual task is involved. Our ethical obligation is to speak so as to respect the integrity of those with whom we talk and to create optimal conditions for self-expression. In purposive discussion the same requirements exist, but added to them is the obligation to speak so as to contribute most fully to the fulfillment of the intellectual task at hand.

Work relationships. This general category is intended to include situations in which there is a hierarchy of authority and the need for cooperative action. Much has been written about personnel relationships and the principles of communication that underlie cooperative and efficient work. The fundamental concern has ordinarily been the success of particular business organizations, but the overall results have generally been valuable for the people affected and for the society as a whole. Ethical standards have been raised.

Work relationships involve authority relationships that provide opportunities for those at higher levels in the hierarchy to take advantage of those at lower levels. In the superior–subordinate relationship there are built-in ego-defense problems. Whether these problems are exploited or minimized depends mainly upon the superior's understanding of himself and his subordinates, his understanding of communication, and his ethical standards. Too often a person in a position of authority uses his prerogatives for the enhancement of his own ego, often at the expense of those over whom he exercises his authority. Arbitrary orders, inconsistent demands, inadequate information, discrimination, unfair appraisal, and tactlessness are among the affronts the personality of a subordinate may receive. Unfortunately, some of these may be done without the superior being aware of what he is doing. In such cases the understanding of self is particularly important to the superior's morally good actions.

What is said here by no means intended to suggest that there is anything inherently unethical about authority and discipline. Hierarchical structure and authority appear to be essential to human organizations. But if human dignity is to be preserved, the structure must be flexible enough to adapt to the changing needs of people, and the authority limited, conditional, and exercised with prudence.

Human values are best served in the communications of work relations when such ethical obligations as the following are recognized: When someone is instructing, he is obligated to be as thoroughly informed and prepared as possible, so that he can teach most effectively, and he must preserve the self-esteem of those he instructs. When one has orders to give, the orders must be as carefully planned as possible and given in such a way as to maintain the self-respect of him who receives them, and to provide whatever opportunities exist for his development. Likewise, criticism should be given so that the subordinate's self-esteem is preserved. Channels of communication based on lines of authority must be respected so that the position of intermediate personnel is not undermined. Information that will be useful must not be withheld. Opportunities for communication on the part of the subordinate must be preserved. In management–employee conferences the trappings of democracy should not be maintained at the expense of the substance of democracy. Men at all levels must assume responsibility for communicating in such a way as to maximize cooperation and productivity.

The structure of any organization is a complex web of communications. Especially is this true of a business or industrial organization, where intricate coordination of many activities is essential. Only insofar as conscientious efforts are made to preserve the integrity of every personality, at every level of the organization, are moral obligations being fulfilled.

Related readings

Barnlund, Dean C. **Interpersonal Communication: Survey and Studies.** Boston: Houghton-Mifflin, 1968. Pp. 613–719.

Childs, Marquis W., and Douglass Cater. **Ethics in a Business Society.** New York: Mentor Books (New American Library of World Literature), 1954.

Ginnott, Haim G. **Between Parent and Child.** New York: Avon Books, 1965.

Smith, T. V., and William Debbins. **Constructive Ethics.** Englewood Cliffs, N.J.: Prentice-Hall, 1948.

SIX

"In times like these..."

Erich Kahler's words, quoted in the preface to this volume, come to mind again as we consider how we are going to go about developing our ethical sense and sharpening our ethical judgment: "In times like these, decent behavior is no simple matter, for it is no longer merely a moral, but also a mental, task. It requires a highly developed intellectual faculty, the ability to grasp the very complex social situation of a closely interrelated nation and world. . . ." Kahler, of course, goes far beyond the concerns of this book, but his statement helps to pose our problem for us.

A predisposition to do good—indeed, a will to do good growing out of genuine concern—is necessary for morally right conduct, but it is not sufficient given the circumstances of the modern world. The changing and increasingly complex relationships among men require a constant reinterpretation of values and the application of ethical principles to new circumstances. Thus more and more information and critical evaluation are needed, and more thoughtful appraisal of the consequences of individual and social actions. Intellectual development thus becomes a part of our moral development.

Beyond this, moral action requires imaginative sympathy, a quality of thought that depends upon both moral and intellectual factors as well as upon emotional sensitivity. We must be able to sense, to understand, to appreciate how others may be affected by our words and actions. As the relationships among people become more complex and the effects of actions more far-reaching, we must become more imaginatively sympathetic. And our concern must extend farther and farther beyond our immediate group to the larger community.

In view of the difficulty of moral behavior in modern life, it is unfortunate that a situation exists which led a former president of one of our great universities to say that "Formal education in the United States has given relatively slight attention to the development of moral intelligence. There has been a disposition in many quarters to say that this is not a responsibility of formal education, or that moral intelligence cannot be had by means of formal education."[1] Another university president says, "There are many who seem to say that the university . . . is concerned solely with matters of the intellect (as if intellect were a separate and unrelated entity possessed by man), and that matters of virtue or of goodness or of ethical conduct are personal matters which lie outside the province of the university."[2]

Traditionally in our society moral training has been the responsibility of the home and the church. It seems fair to say that our religious institutions have tended to monopolize moral training on the assumption that morality is fundamentally religious in nature, or that the only legitimate basis of moral principles lies in religion. Secular schools, separated from the church by law, have not been thought of as bearing a responsibility for ethical training except insofar as they encourage honesty, industry, and sportsmanship. There is more than the religious bias involved, however. Serious discussion of ethical standards and their application in the life of the individual and society inevitably result in the calling into question of socially sanctioned institutions, certain laws and their enforcement, the distribution of wealth, discrimination, political campaigning, the conduct of public office, and the general conduct of life in society. Such discussion and the controversy it entails are too often shunned by the public schools (below the college level, and sometimes even there) in the interest of maintaining good relationships with parents and the

[1] Edmund E. Day, **Education for Freedom and Responsibility** (Ithaca: Cornell University Press, 1952), pp. 70–71.
[2] Murray G. Ross, "Ethical Goals of Modern Education," in **A Humane Society**, ed. Stuart Rosenberg (Toronto: University of Toronto Press, 1962), p. 28.

community in general. Serious discussion of such issues is too often shunned by the community itself, since many of its members have vested interests in traditional economic, political, religious, and racial relationships.

At the college level, of course, ethics is a formal study, and there is much discussion of ethical theory, and some discussion of its relationship to current affairs. There is, however, too much of a tendency to relegate ethical considerations to the formal courses in ethics alone, rather than to consider ethical issues whenever they are relevant. That is not to say that ethical prescriptions are to be laid down for students and teachers. It is to say that ethical problems posed by economic, political, and social policy should be rigorously examined, and the importance of a sense of moral responsibility and commitment emphasized.

The contributors to **Prospect for America,** in their discussion of motivations and values, set the tone for an approach to ethics in the general classroom:

> We would not wish to impose upon students a rigidly defined commitment. But this freedom must be understood in its true light. We believe that the individual should be free and morally responsible: the two are inseparable. The fact that we tolerate differing values must not be confused with moral neutrality. Such tolerance must be built upon a base of moral commitment; otherwise it degenerates into a flaccid indifference, purged of all belief and devotion.[3]

There is room for such an approach in every classroom where human problems are discussed.

There has been in recent years an increasing concern over the moral level of conduct in our society. Searching questions have been asked, seeking causes and solutions. Traditional values have eroded, or are inadequate—as currently interpreted—for the new conditions we experience. To be sure, it is one of the heartening signs of the times that there is significant moral ferment taking place in our society. There is growing moral indignation at the exploitation of our human and natural resources and at the inequality and injustices that have been visited upon so many of our fellowmen. And beyond that, indignation at the lack of opportunity for development, for the

[3] **Prospect for America: The Rockefeller Reports** (Garden City, N.Y.: Doubleday, 1961), p. 392.

achievement of a better quality of life, which lack grows in large part out of our misplaced priorities.

It is one of the anomalies of human conduct, however, that moral concern not infrequently shows itself in actions that seem to contradict the very principles and ends held up as the moral commitment. It is perhaps not too difficult to understand how this can be when, for example, frustrations over prolonged injustice goad one to strike out to shatter the complacent face of authority that does not respond. It is only too true that in our society significant reforms usually come after tragedy has stirred the public conscience. The processes of democracy through which we seek social change as well as stability are complex, and sometimes largely immobilized by the many conflicting demands of citizen groups. We have not as yet in our society reached sufficiently wide agreement on moral priorities to make our democratic system adequately responsive to social needs. But respond it does when we direct majority opinion in a particular direction; it is unfortunate that this too often must happen in the wake of the tragic circumstance we could have foreseen, and usually have.

Moral judgment, then, is made more difficult by the fact that we often have conduct that is essentially selfless, but which uses illegal and/or what we would ordinarily consider unethical means to achieve what are believed to be ethical ends. We have seen the encouragement of draft evasion and the burning of draft cards to promote opposition to a war; the disruption of community life and the destruction of property to hasten social reform; the shouting down of a speaker whose views are seen as representing an immoral establishment. To be sure, it is not always possible to determine to what degree such behavior may be essentially self-serving, despite the moral claims.

What is more prevalent, of course, is the use of legal and ostensibly democratic means to achieve selfish ends, and this often with a pious declaration of faith in and devotion to democratic virtues.

When we are committed to what we believe are highly moral ends, it is easy to argue that the ends justify the means. And, plainly, in a sense they do. If the ends do not justify the means, what does? But what is usually overlooked, or at least considered much the lesser evil perhaps because less obvious, is that the means themselves bring about certain ends—the means have effects of their own. For example, repeated violation of law, even in the pursuit of noble ends, may well foster a disrespect for law; and surely a respect for law is essential to the successful functioning of a civilized society. Discriminatory laws also foster a disrespect for law, but this circumstance does not invalidate the other.

Moreover, not only do the means have effects in themselves, but the means almost certainly shape the goal they were originally designed to achieve. It is difficult to see, for instance, how a political campaign that is carried on with false accusations, with appeals to prejudice, and with the obfuscation of issues can avoid not only weakening the democratic process as a means of selecting leadership, but also altering the very concept and function of the political office which it fills. A political office, after all, is what it is and functions as it does largely because of the conception citizens have of it. Disrespect for the office, a lack of confidence in it as embodied in a particular person, cannot but significantly alter the role of that office, its capacity to fulfill its obligations. And it is difficult to believe that a man who gets accustomed to the use of unethical means to get into office will completely eschew such means once he arrives.

Such considerations as these make us increasingly aware of how carefully and thoughtfully ethical judgments must be made. It is plainly impossible in many, if not in most, instances to determine whether on balance the good that the sought-for ends have achieved outweighs the ill effects of the means used. In an earlier chapter we discussed this problem with respect to methods of persuasion that foster overemotional decision making. Establishing highly emotionalized decision making as a norm would hardly be desirable, nor would establishing the use of force as a means of social change. In this volume we are asking whether the means and ends in the long run foster the optimum growth of human personalities. The question is much easier to ask than to answer.

It seems difficult to deny that at times in our history the use of coercive power has been morally justified in the redress of wrongs. It is hard to imagine a more morally justifiable application of pressure to force a reluctant choice than that applied by the blacks who boycotted the Birmingham bus system and forced it by economic pressure to change its discriminatory policy. Various strikes by laboring groups in the past have forced employers to share more equitably the value created by the workers' labor and to improve working conditions. Labor unions have at times, it also seems plain, used coercive power to gain questionable advantages while creating economic and social problems for other groups. This cannot be considered a justifiable use of coercive power. Further, the destruction of property or the injuring of a person cannot, from the perspective of this volume, be justified, except in self-defense.

One might argue, of course, that the best defense is a good offense, and it is conceivable that offensive action in a limited way might be justified, but this imposes a great moral burden on the initiator. One might also argue that established economic and political institutions have a vast array of subtle ways of coercion, and that the more direct assault on the part of individual citizens or a group of citizens can be justified because they have no other way of achieving their objectives. Again, such circumstances arise, but here again a great moral burden is assumed by the one who insists that the means of nondestructive action and pressure have been exhausted.

What makes these issues of crucial importance in the consideration of the ethics of speech communication is that ultimately, if we cannot discuss our mutual problems, if we cannot through the use of language analyze our social problems and reach workable agreements on courses of action to create acceptable social conditions, then the only recourse is to force. If force becomes the principle of social change, we are in danger of destroying the foundations upon which we can build a community in which freedom and self-determination can have meaning. Destructive force adopted as a means of social change tends to escalate as it triggers deep emotions, limits the alternatives open for action, and often evokes counter forces equally or more destructive. That destructive force will occasionally be unleashed in every human society is perhaps inevitable for the foreseeable future of man, but to legitimize it in social action is to erode man's dignity and integrity, and is contrary to the principle of self-determination— it is incompatible with a democratic society.

The intention here is not to overemphasize the ethical problems attendant upon the abandonment of persuasion for coercion. But the degree to which protest and activism, indeed outright violence, have characterized our society during the past decade makes it important that we carefully consider the ethical implications of coercion, and thus be better prepared in the future to make ethical distinctions and decisions.

Surely it is in the classrooms of our colleges and high schools, and particularly the communication classrooms, that the ethical aspects of communication and issues related to it should be discussed. The scope of ethical questions is enormous, ranging from those arising out of the interpersonal interactions of everyday life, through those of the community and the nation, to the larger world society. In this volume an attempt has been made to point up ethical problems in communication, open up avenues for exploration, and suggest broad criteria for ethical evaluation without, however, attempting to cover the whole range of possibilities.

It would doubtless be well for all of us as we prepare to analyze the ethical quality of the communications we experience to look at ourselves as students and teachers and the way we ourselves talk and interact with others. In the preceding chapter we briefly discussed the ethics of interpersonal communication. We can all ask ourselves how well we measure up to the criteria that call for deep respect for other human personalities, especially when we have an abiding dislike for the views they hold and express. And we can ask how well we create conditions that open up channels of communication and maintain the integrity of the other selves; how readily we pretend to understand when we really don't; how readily we discuss a problem following the conventions of organized discussion without ever coming to grips with the significant issues; how readily we define and redefine, and obfuscate so as to avoid meeting an issue or conceding a point; how readily we say one thing to our fellow students or instructors in the classroom and something quite different outside; how readily we as teachers give a validity that is unwarranted to a theory we like, and derogate the one we do not like; how readily we put on fronts, and avoid basic controversies to keep our academic and social worlds tidy; how readily academic success for the student and professional success for the teacher lead to the expedient rather than the important. We can answer these questions only for ourselves as individuals, but asking them marks the growth of genuine concern for more ethical speech.

Since we live in a world of words, and communication is an ever-present aspect of our lives in every phase of activity, the communications needing evaluation are almost coextensive with our communicative behavior. The classroom, especially if there is active student participation, provides much opportunity for the discussion and application of ethical principles. Too often we see the classroom as a place apart from the "real world." We use the classroom as a base for assessing what goes on in the rest of society, and indeed we should. But to make ethical issues most meaningful, we need to consider critically the moral quality of the communications in and related to the work of each course of study. Certainly if we can analyze and evaluate other qualities of performance, we should also be able to analyze and evaluate the ethical quality of the communication taking place. The preceding chapters should provide a basis for such evaluation.

When we do look at society beyond the classroom we find such a bewildering array of communications from so many sources, in so many media, directed toward so many and such diverse ends, interacting and conflicting, that it is difficult to know where to begin: Advertising, of course, is an obvious form of persuasive communication, much criticized for questionable ethical standards; political speeches at all levels; speeches by leaders of the multitudinous organizations of our society, business, labor, professional, service—their numbers are legion; also preaching, talk shows, public discussions, interviews, commentaries—we are bombarded with an incredible volume of talk. But these are only the more obvious communications; there are others of equal or greater concern: the realm of public information, from both private and government sources; the negotiations among the numerous power groups, not only in government but in business, labor, and professional organizations; the endless hearings and discussions that precede the passing of legislation; the subtle persuasions of government in all its branches at its various levels; the procedures and persuasions in courts of law; all of these must continuously be scrutinized and subjected to moral judgment.

All communications, of course, cannot be subjected to public scrutiny. Inevitably some of the affairs of men must be privileged; there must be discretion used in laying bare the talk and actions of any individual or group. But while this is recognized, the problem of secrecy itself is an ethical issue and must be thoughtfully evaluated as a part of the ethical problems of communication in society.

The use of language as such, both in written and spoken forms, should be of particular concern in our ethical evaluations. The protest movements of the past decade and the reactions to them seem to have generated a peculiar denigration of language as a means to interaction and cooperation.[4] We have heard from the campus and the street, as well as from the political platform, that it is time to quit talking and start acting, apparently on the assumption that action does not need to be planned, evaluated, directed, and reevaluated through the use of language. That language can confuse, and indeed can be used to avoid action, in no way decreases the importance of the intelligent use of words in social change.

Our words have effects on people, on them as personalities and on the affairs they and we conduct. There are words whose effects are subtle and unperceived; there are words that comfort and words that pain, that support and that undermine; words that inform and that mislead, that foster rationality and that impede it; words that unite and words that divide.

Whenever we choose words with which to speak we make a moral judgment, because our decision has some impact on human personalities—interest meets interest; the path of one unit of life is crossed by that of another.

The orientation of this book has been toward democratic values. While based on a commitment to a certain concept of the nature of man, democratic values are largely procedural. That is, democratic values do not prescribe for men **what** they should believe or do, but rather **how** they should go about deciding what to believe or do. The assumption is that freedom of thought and expression, freedom for discussion and debate, for inquiry, criticism, and choice, coupled with respect for the integrity of all men, will bring about the optimum development of human personality.

It no longer suffices, however, that we accept freedom of speech and accept democratic procedure and discipline as things given and self-perpetuating. Freedom must be deliberately cultivated, and democratic procedure and discipline carefully fostered and strengthened, and the opportunity for self-determination enhanced wherever possible. These characteristics of a free community become more and more difficult to preserve and enlarge in an increasingly massive, complex, and technologized society.

All of the student's work in the humane studies should increase his

---

[4] See the discussion of the use of language on the campus in James A. Michener, **Kent State: What Happened and Why** (New York: Random House, 1971), pp. 241–245. Michener's entire book is recommended for students interested in the problems and ethics of communication.

understanding of the problems of freedom and self-determination. As Ralph Barton Perry said, "I define 'the humanities,' then, to embrace whatever influences conduce to freedom." And he adds, "By freedom, . . . I mean the exercise of enlightened choice. I mean the action in which habit, reflex or suggestion is superseded by an individual's fundamental judgments of good and evil; the action whose premises are explicit; the action which proceeds from personal reflection and the integration of interests."[5] The concept of freedom must be developed throughout the broad range of a liberal education.

Related readings

Auer, J. Jeffrey. **The Rhetoric of Our Times.** New York: Meredith Corporation, 1969.

Bay, Christian. **The Structure of Freedom.** New York: Atheneum Books, 1968. [Originally published by Stanford University Press, 1958.]

Bosmajian, Haig A., ed. **The Principles and Practice of Freedom of Speech.** Boston: Houghton Mifflin, 1971.

Lippmann, Walter. **The Public Philosophy.** New York: Mentor Books, 1955.

Parson, Donn W., and Wil A. Linkugel, eds. **Militancy and Anti-Communication.** Proceedings of the Second Annual Symposium on Issues in Public Communication, University of Kansas, 1969.

Skolnick, Jerome H. **The Politics of Protest.** New York: Ballantine Books, 1969. The Skolnick Report to The National Commission on the Causes and Prevention of Violence.

[5] Ralph Barton Perry, **The Humanity of Man** (New York: George Braziller, 1956), p. 26.

Index of Names

Auer, J. Jeffrey, 106
Axtelle, George E., 93

Baier, Kurt, 20, 85
Baker, George P., 69
Barnlund, Dean C., 96
Bay, Christian, 106
Benne, Kenneth D., 93
Berlo, David K., 48
Bonhoeffer, Dietrich, 24
Bosmajian, Haig A., 106
Brandt, Richard B., 20
Brown, Charles T., 20
Brown, James A. C., 49, 83

Cater, Douglas, 96
Chesebro, James W., 20
Childs, Marquis W., 96

Dahl, Robert, 73
Day, Edmund E., 42, 98
Debbins, William, 20, 87, 96

Evjen, Henry O., 81, 82

Fearnside, W. Ward, 83
Fletcher, Joseph, 20
Fortas, Abe, 16

Foster, William T., 69
Frankel, Charles, 44, 73
Frankena, W. K., 5
Freeley, Austin J., 70

Garnett, A. Campbell, 20, 85, 86
Ginnott, Haim G., 96
Guérard, Albert, 33
Gulley, Halbert E., 48

Haiman, Franklyn S., 20, 83
Halther, William B., 83
Hammarskjöld, Dag, xi, 35, 87
Hastings, Arthur, 70
Hawkins, D. J. B., 85
Hocking, William E., 59
Hollingsworth, Harry L., 16
Hovland, Carl I., 48

Janis, Irving L., 48
Johannesen, Richard, 83

Kahler, Eric, xii, 97
Keller, Paul W., 20
Kelley, Harold H., 48

Levi, Albert W., 20
Linkugel, Wil A., 106

Lippmann, Walter, 106

McBurney, James H., 69, 70
MacIver, R. M., 16
Maslow, Abraham H., 20
Meiklejohn, Alexander, 59
Michener, James A., 105
Mill, John Stuart, 42, 153
Miller, Gerald R., 83
Mills, Glenn E., 69, 70
Milton, John, 44
Minnick, Wayne C., 69
Morgan, A. E., xii, 58, 59
Mumford, Lewis, 59

Nilsen, Thomas R., 59, 83
Nixon, Charles R., 59

Osgood, Charles E., 48
Overstreet, Harry, 89

Parson, Donn W., 106
Perry, Ralph Barton, 4, 44, 54, 106

Rader, Melvin, 18, 86
Randall, John Herman, 25
Raup, R. Bruce, 93
Rosenberg, Stuart, 56, 98
Ross, Murray G., 42, 56, 98
Ruesch, Jurgen, 90

Simon, Yves, 61, 66
Skolnick, Jerome H., 106
Smith, B. Othanel, 93
Smith, T. V., 20, 87, 96
Suci, George J., 48

Tannenbaum, Percy H., 48

Van Doren, Mark, xii

Wallace, Karl, 20
Walter, Otis M., 20
Whitehead, Alfred North, 20
Wieman, Henry N., 20
Windes, Russel R., 70
Wriston, Henry M., 44

Subject Index

Advertisements, 8
Advertising, 9
Ambiguity, 75
Argumentation, 69
   and persuasion, 69, 70
Attitude change, 48, 49

Bad, concept of the, 15
Benevolence, 41

Campaign speaking, 5, 6
Choice, effective, 44
Choice, significant, 46
   and emotion, 57
   and the ethics of speech, 43
   and freedom, 44, 54
   and the market place of ideas, 53
   and motivation to, 55
   and rationality, 43
   and self-understanding, 55
Coercion, 61, 66, 67, 68, 101
Communication, interpersonal,
      11, 19, 88
   in an institutional context, 37
Congruity principles, 48
Conversation and discusion, 92

Emotional appeals, 48

Ethical
   issues and reasoning, 78 ff.
   judgments, bases of, 11 ff.
   problems in communication, 5 ff.
   requirements of speech, 18
Ethics
   of conversation and discussion,
      92 ff.
   deontological, 4
   in education, 98, 99
   of information, 38, 71
   of interpersonal relations, 88 ff.
   of reasoning, 76 ff.
   teleological, 4
   of work relations, 94 ff.

Fallacies, definition of, 80
   types of, 80, 81
Falsehood, 22
Force, 102
Freedom, 44, 54, 106
   of thought, 65

Good, concept of the, 15

Honesty, 39

Impartial good will, 86

Inference levels, 77
Information
  amount of, 37, 38
  ethics of, 71 ff.
  management of, 37
Interpersonal and family relation-
    ships, 88 ff.

Justice, 41

Language, 25, 26, 40, 65, 67, 104
Law, and freedom of thought, 65
  violation of, 16, 68, 100
Listeners' responsibility, 74
Logical appeals, 48, 49

Man, concept of, 14
Meanings, of words, 75
Minorities, 10
Moral decision, 15
  obligations, 61, 65, 74, 85, 95
Morality, definition of, 15
  and intention, 15, 17
Morals, xii

News management, 36
Newspaper reporting, 8
Nonlogical appeals, 49
Nonmoral, definition of, 15

Obligatory, the, 85
Optimific act, 85
Ought, feelings of, 3
  esthetic, 16
  legal, 16
  moral, 16
  prudential, 16

Pentagon Papers, 35
Persuasion, definitions of, 60, 61
  and coercion, 61, 66–68
  constituents of, 68 ff.
  and democracy, 61

  and ethical principles, 61
  means of, 65, 71
  and moral obligations, 61, 65 ff.
Political campaigns, 2
President's Commission on
    National Goals, 44
Pressure groups, 10
Propaganda, definition of, 81
  and coercion, 66
  devices of, 81, 82
  messages, 49
  and persuasion, 66
Prospect for America, 99
Protest, 7, 67

Reasoning
  errors in, 60 ff.
  ethics of, 76 ff.
  in persuasion, 78 ff.
Right, concept of the, 15

Secrecy, 35, 37

Television programs, 8
Trial procedure, 37
Truth
  of discourse, 28, 34
  and emotions, 32
  and literary art, 33
  of the situation, 30, 41
  on trying to tell the truth, 40
Truth telling, concept of, 22, 27
  and the institutional context, 37
  and news management, 37
  values and language, 22
Truthfulness and honesty, 39

Value assumptions, 76

Word meanings, 75
Work relationships, 94
Wrong, concept of the, 15